SO-AHC-692

Life After Death

Other Books by Skip Crayton

REMEMBER WHEN

THE LETTER SWEATER

Life After Death

BY

SKIP CRAYTON

McBryde Publishing
NEW BERN, NORTH CAROLINA USA

NEW BERN, NORTH CAROLINA USA

LIFE AFTER DEATH
Copyright © 2011 by Skip Crayton

All rights reserved. No part of this book may be reproduced in any form or by any electronic or mechanical means, including information storage or retrieval systems, without permission in writing from the publisher, except by a reviewer who may quote brief passages in a review.

www.mcbrydepublishing.com

Cover by Bill Benners
Interior Layout by Bill Benners
10 9 8 7 6 5 4 3 2 1

ISBN 978-0-9829946-8-9

First Printing August 1, 2011
Printed in the United States of America

Dedication

*M*ARY RUTH CRAYTON was born on July 5, 1972. She died just seven short days later. With her death, the chance that I might have a son or daughter died with her. That day, a part of me left the world forever. On Father's Day, 2006, that part of me that had been gone for so long, burst back into my heart.

Just weeks before, I had asked Sam, my wife Carol's son, if he'd allow me to adopt him. I told him that he could keep his name, but if he said yes, he would be my son forever. I also told him that if it was something he did not want to do, rather than to struggle with having to tell me no, he could just never bring up the subject again and I would understand.

About a month passed and I had no answer. I was beginning to think that Sam had decided against the adoption. After lunch on Father's Day, as I finished opening the usual cards from my dogs and cats, Sam reached over and handed me one last card. Trembling, I opened the card and immediately "lost it." Written in Sam's handwriting, just under the verse was: *The answer is Yes! I Love You.*

If I had asked God to send me a son, he would have sent me Samuel Jackson Dail.

Sam, this book is dedicated to you...I Love You.

Acknowledgements

ONE WOULD THINK that writing my third book would be a breeze. But it has been anything but a breeze. At times, tackling this story has been more like the storm Jack faced in my second book *The Letter Sweater*. And at other times, it has been an emotional roller coaster. Unlike in fiction, where I have the liberty of changing the story as I go or to follow the whims of my characters, I knew all too well how this story would play out because it is my story.

That being said, I still needed help. Throughout the three years it took to write and rewrite *Life After Death*, there were many who lent a helping hand along the way. That help came in many forms, from simple things like helping me to remember a detail or date, to complex things like making sure my understanding of Christian theology was solid. And there were those who acted as cheerleaders, encouraging me along the way.

Jimmy and Patti Jones, you have been my angels along the way. And I am so blessed to have friends like Annie and Larry Parker, Bob and Missy Baskerville, Bill and Dorrie Benners, Fred and Bea Hessick, Ron Moore and Allee Humphrey along with the others who reached out and helped God carry me through my darkest hour.

I cannot forget my family—my nephew Glenn and his wife Christine, my niece Debbie and her husband Robin, my brother Frank and his wife Dana—your support was never ending. And, of course, my sister Debby—my pillar of strength and guardian angel.

Jane could not have had better doctors both in New Bern and in Chapel Hill, but two stand out from the rest. Ron Moore may be the smartest doctor to ever wear a white coat. He is not only a great doctor, he is a very close friend. David Byrd is not just a great doctor, he is one of the most compassionate people I've ever had the privilege to know. God blessed us far beyond anything either of us deserved by placing Jane's care in the hands of those two wonderful doctors.

My knowledge of *The Bible* is far from complete. The reason that I wrote *Life After Death* was a burning desire to give hope to those who go through the loss of a loved one. It is my intention that my story might give a ray of inspiration or maybe even lead a brokenhearted soul to God. In order for me to make sure that my theology was on solid ground, I sought the advice of five people with firm theological backgrounds. Each read the manuscript and helped me to make sure that I was headed in the right direction. My heartfelt thanks go out to Steve Cobb, Lloyd Griffith, Doug Stewart, Jane Merritt, John Check and Powell Osteen.

Recently, Carol and I were invited to a small dinner party at the governor's mansion in Raleigh. Before we sat down, we were treated to a tour of the upstairs residence, a place few North Carolinians will ever see. While the Governor was showing the others one bedroom, her husband Bob took me to another and pointed to the bed he slept in as a young boy. A tear slipped down my check as I looked at him and said. "Yes, Bob. I know. I slept in that same bed for almost three weeks when Jane was at Chapel Hill." Bob's face flushed. "I'd almost forgotten that." Bob Eaves and Bev Perdue offered me their full measure of love and friendship during the hardest time of my life and I can never thank them enough.

I cannot thank Bill Benners enough. Not only is he the best editor I know (both book and film, I might add), he is the best at everything he does. He is also a best friend. Bill, you nailed the cover design.

A special thanks to my colleague Debbie Wallis. Last year, I taught you to write. This year, the student became the teacher. Thanks for all you did.

I would also like to thank the new Jane in my life and soon to be daughter-in-law, Jane Moon. Girl, I love you and look forward to holding my grandbabies.

There are four women who have made a huge impact on my life and I feel a real need to single them out. Each lived through a depression and survived a world war. Each raised families and lived what they would call ordinary lives, but each in a way had an extraordinary effect on my life—Vivian Cox, Jane's mother; Estelle Dail, Carol's mother; Flossie Crayton, my mother; and Pat Jones, my "other" mother.

And then there's God and my family. Carol and Sam are the rays of sunshine that brighten the weariest of days. They complete me. And God, what would I be without You? Maybe one day I'll learn to not just listen to what You say, but to finally learn that all I have to do when tough times happen is to place it all in Your hands. You bless me by loving me.

Life After Death

PART ONE

"What it's all about is not just a moment of pleasure on our journey to Heaven, but the journey itself. What it is all about is Kingdom Living now."

—Dr. Steve Cobb
Pastor, Temple Baptist Church
New Bern, North Carolina

Prologue

HE DRUMMING THUMP of the helicopter blades beat a deafening rhythm as I stood in the parking lot of Pitt Memorial Hospital, waiting for the chopper to lift off. The scene, eerie and not unlike something out of *Apocalypse Now* or *Platoon*, a scene from a war I was blessed to avoid, reminded me of a similar day in my life, a déjà vu that had haunted me for years.

Standing beside me as we watched, hoping to see the airborne ambulance that would take my precious Jane to the hospital in Chapel Hill, was my sister Debby and Jane's old college friend Peggy. Off to the right, holding on to each other and staring into the sky as if awaiting the shuttle to blast into space, stood my brother Frank and his wife Dana, all of us holding our breath and fighting back tears hoping that God would grant us another miracle.

Only moments before, I had signed a form allowing the transfer to take place, a form that told me that Jane was considered too unstable for the trip and letting me know that she might not make it to the hospital where her only chance for life would be a transplant. For more than three years, Jane had been on the liver transplant list. But that organ would have to take a back seat to what she needed now—a heart.

The slow thumping of the blades grew louder and louder until they turned into a high-pitched roar, echoing off the building, the parking lot and even the trees. Finally, the dark blue helicopter with "EastCare" scrawled across the side appeared, hovering slowly as it climbed above the main building. Seconds later, it turned westward and darted away like a shooting star. This would be Jane's second trip in such a vehicle and, like her first helicopter ride, one she would never remember.

Chapter
1

I USED TO NEVER WAKE at six-thirty, especially on a Sunday morning. Something urged me to stir that morning of June 2, 2001. It could have been a sound or maybe a feeling, but it was unlike anything I'd ever experienced. Something, or someone I'd later relate to as an angel, had awakened me. Before that day, angels had existed in other people's thoughts, but not in mine. But the sound or feeling that brought me to my senses was unlike anything I'd ever experienced and since that day, it has never happened again.

The night before, my wife Jane had fallen into a state of mind called encephalopathy, a confusion-like state caused by her liver's inability to expel ammonia from her blood stream. In its mildest form, encephalopathy would affect her mind making it difficult to remember things like birthdays or names. In its extreme form, it can rage into a coma-like state. Because of her confused condition, and fearing that she might get out of bed during the night, get lost and stumble down the stairs, I'd decided that we'd sleep downstairs on the twin couches that faced each other in our family room.

Whatever it was that had awakened me had not left me feeling fearful and for a moment or two I laid on the

17

couch, enjoying the warmth of my dog, Little Mutt, as she snuggled against my legs. At first, I felt content and one with the world. Seconds later that feeling shivered away like a blast of icy wind on a winter's day. When I opened my eyes, I froze. What I saw just a few feet across from me on the other couch terrified me. I couldn't believe my eyes. I saw Jane lying on her back, her eyes glazed in a fixed stare as she ingested her own vomit.

"Jane!" I shouted. "Jane! Wake up!"

She did not move as she continued to swallow her vomit.

I leapt from the couch, knocking Little Mutt to the floor, "Wake up," I cried. "Oh God, make her wake up."

What took place over the next few minutes remains more of a dream to me than reality, much of it in slow motion. I've always been proud that I am an Eagle Scout and I guess much of that training took over as I fell into a state of automatic pilot. I reached down Jane's throat and cleared her air passage. Still she did not move, her arms hanging off the couch like limp rags. I rolled her onto her stomach and pounded on her back. Still nothing.

Fear grabbed hold of me as if I'd stumbled onto a robber in a dark alley. But it was not fear for me, it was fear for Jane. I realized at that moment that my precious Jane might die. Trembling, I looked around the room as if I was looking for help. I placed my hand to my mouth and took a deep breath. *Ron Moore*, I thought. A quick call to Jane's doctor found him awake and on call. Without hesitation, he told me to call 911; he'd see me at the hospital.

THE EARLY MORNING SUNLIGHT crept under the portico changing its incandescent yellow to a florescent white as it filtered into the antiseptic loneliness of the emergency room. On one wall, children's paintings hung in an effort to cheer those who really didn't care. And on another, a blank television stared across the room, its unlit blue-green screen adding to the desolation I felt. Being alone is a dreadful thing, especially when you are afraid. And thinking straight is even more difficult. With the adrenaline flow dissipated and Jane finally at the hospital, I sat alone with my fears. Since we didn't have children, my wife had always been the most important human being in my life. The thought of losing her ripped at my heart, bringing back the buried pain from the loss of our only child. All I could do was sit and stare at the walls and pray. With my mother and brother out of town and Jane's mom too feeble to call, I needed someone. But who could I call? Ron Moore, Jane's doctor and one of my closest friends was with her, but all he'd told me was that he was going to put her on a ventilator. After that I hadn't seen him and anyway, I wanted him with her not me. *Who could I call?* I kept asking myself.

I guess Jimmy Jones is the closest person to me in the entire world. I cannot remember a time in my life when he was not in it. Other than the fact that we have different parents, he "is" my brother. For much of my life this five-foot-six-inch "giant" of a man with snow-white hair had been my number one confident; the person I trusted the most other than Jane. And his wife, Patti, stood right beside him in my pecking order of fiends.

Sometimes it is difficult for a man to have a close female friend, especially with someone who is blonde and "Marilyn Monroe" gorgeous. She and I had had a close relationship long before she and Jimmy had married after the death of his first wife. Patti was one of Jane's best friends and there was never an ounce of jealously between the two of them as far as I was concerned.

19

I knew they were spending the weekend at their summer place and a part of me didn't want to make the call, yet I longed for someone to hold my heart and to help me grab hold of my senses. So I made the call. As I told Jimmy what had happened, I could hear Patti telling him to get a move on it. A sigh of relief flushed over me, yet I also knew it would be an hour or more before they could get to me.

Emergency rooms are a strange place and the one at Craven Regional Medical Center is no different than any in small town America. With the trauma of Saturday night knifings and gunshot wounds over, the Sunday morning at New Bern's only hospital took on a surreal mood. As I sat in the far corner, my back against the huge glass windows that faced the alleyway, the activities seemed almost dreamlike. There were no comings and goings. Only the receptionist making work for herself as she sat at her desk in the center of the room while a homeless man used the telephone, and a family sat huddled together a few feet away from me.

As I waited, my thoughts raced back to the weeks and months before when Jane had been diagnosed with liver failure; the trips to the hospitals both at New Bern and in Chapel Hill, her pain and anguish, watching her as she wasted away to almost nothing. And the bouts she had with encephalopathy, the commitment we had both made that we were going to beat this thing and get her on the liver transplant list no matter how long it took. Confusing thoughts stirred back and forth until my brain felt like mush.

The minutes trickled by as I sat there in my loneliness. Over an hour had passed yet nothing around me had changed. No one else had broken the spell that seemed to exist in that room; the same people were there as if they were a part of some Rod Serling teleplay. Ron had not been back to let me know what was happening. My sadness deepened and the tears I'd fought all morning started to trickle, then flow down my cheeks. Terrified, I hurt beyond all measure.

For some reason the homeless man across the room captured my attention and my sadness turned to anger as I watched him. I found it impossible to comprehend how the hospital could allow this person to make phone call after phone call to whomever he pleased as if the phone he was using belonged to him personally. He stood defiantly across the room calling everyone he seemed to know and talking at the top of his voice while hospital workers walked passed him, ignoring his very existence. *How dare they be so insensitive!* I thought. Here I am with my wife's life hanging by a thread and they allow this person to invade my space with his constant chatter.

"Go find a payphone," I wanted to shout.

I took a deep breath and closed my eyes as my sadness engulfed my anger. I forgot about the rude caller and blocked him from my thoughts. What caught my attention was a moment of light that will live with me forever. My gaze fell upon the family at the other end of the room. Their laughter and togetherness appeared so out of place in the morgue-like atmosphere of the emergency room. Yet, unlike the caller, they did not offend me. It was as if they had a warm glow encircling them that brightened the corner where they gathered. I could almost see the light that surrounded them and feel its warmth as it seemed to pull me towards them like a tractor beam.

If there had ever been a perfect television family, it would have probably been the Andersons of *Father Knows Best.* Thoughts of Jim and Betty and their three kids kept seeping into my mind, and I smiled for just a second through my tears. But unlike the Andersons, there was one big difference about these wonderful people whom I knew loved each other and were a real American family, they were African Americans. Seeing

21

them that day removed any stereotype I could have ever had. What happened next was a gift of ministry that swelled my heart and gave me hope. Holding hands, they walked to the door, all smiles. Just as they reached the door, the father whispered something to his wife then turned and walked to me.

I watched him turn and come toward me, expecting him to pass by as if he'd left something behind. When he stopped in front of me, I cocked my head as if to ask why.

The man took my hand and spoke. Because of my emotional state, remembering what he actually said to me has long disappeared. It was as if he spoke to me with his eyes. What I heard sounded something like this, "I hope everything works out for you and your wife. We'll be praying for you both."

"Thank you," I said.

The man smiled, turned and walked through the door. I never saw that man or his family again. But I knew that for the second time that day, God had sent me an angel.

Chapter 2

*T*IME CRAWLED as I sat in the corner, my memories and fears exchanging places like flashbacks from an old movie. I wondered why it was taking so long, but then I wondered was it really taking long or had I just lost track of time. I felt suspended in both time and space. From out of nowhere I felt a tap on my shoulder and my eyes focused back on reality. Standing before me I saw Jimmy. I stared at his moving lips but never heard—no—never understood what he said. I centered my gaze on his eyes and they told me things were bad. When I finally tuned him in, he told me that he'd been looking for me and that they'd already moved Jane to ICU. Immediately I knew that was not good. Only a few years earlier, I had watched my father's pleading eyes as he begged us to unhook the wires that were keeping him alive. *Was I going to face that again?* I thought. My knees wobbled and I found it impossible to stand.

Jimmy grabbed my arm, steadying me as he looked into my eyes. "Hurry, we've got to get upstairs. David Byrd's with her and he needs to talk to you, now." Dr. David Byrd was a dynamo in his late thirties. His goatee offset his shaved head, which housed one of the sharpest brains I'd ever encountered. Raised in Miami near the infamous "South Beach" and educated in Birmingham, he and his wonderful family are a perfect fit in our eastern Carolina community. Dr. Byrd is a

23

man in touch with God. He is probably one of the most spiritual men I've ever known, but at that time I didn't know it. He'd been Jane's liver doctor for just under a year and I had no clue how special he would become in both our lives. My first lesson was getting ready to start.

ICU at Craven Regional Medical Center was just as I had remembered as I peeped through the double doors that only allowed loved ones to enter three times a day. Before I reached the nurses' station, Dr. Byrd pulled me aside and prepared me for what I was about to see. Jane, holding on by a breath, lay across the room; tubes and wires running from her back to the machines that were keeping her alive. A TV screen broadcasted her vitals in bright-green graphics; her heart beating a slow syncopation that my heart desperately kept time with. Each glance toward Jane was followed by one to the screen as if I could pray her heart to keep beating.

"She's in pretty bad shape," Dr. Byrd said. "We can't wait. We've got to get her a liver. I've got to get her to the hospital in Chapel Hill today. They know her there and they have her records. It's our best shot at getting her on a list. Go in and hold her hand and tell her you love her," the doctor said as he motioned toward the room. "I've got the transplant coordinator on the phone. I'll be in in a minute."

"She can hear me?" I asked, my eyes widening.

Dr. Byrd held his hand over the phone. Frowning, he shook his head. "Skip, I don't know. It sure won't hurt. If she can, it will be your voice she wants to hear." His voice trailed off as he focused his attention to the person on the other end who would make the decision whether or not to accept Jane at Chapel Hill.

I looked at my watch expecting it to be some time in the mid-afternoon. Shocked by what I saw; I found it to be just after 10:00 a.m. The day had both flown by and dragged all at the same time. For the first time, fatigue began to set in as I sat next to Jane, holding her hand and praying aloud. *Could it all come down to this?* I thought. In just six days we would celebrate our thirty-fourth wedding anniversary. My heart trembled as I stared at Jane's empty eyes and lifeless-looking body. *Where had all the years gone? What had happened to our plans?* All of it seemed so pointless now as I continued to pray for God to save her and bring her back to me. "This is not supposed to be happening," I silently screamed.

When Dr. Byrd hung up, he motioned for me to follow him. "I need to talk to you," he said as we left the ICU and entered the outside waiting room. As we walked into the drab-green room, Jimmy and Patti perked up, first hugging me, then the doctor. Life is so strange, even weird in the way that it throws things at you. At first it seemed such a cruel coincidence, but as I was to later find out, coincidence is really not a part of our life at all. What was unfolding before me had been planned long before I'd ever been born. Just four short years before, Dr. Byrd had ministered to Jimmy as he faced the loss of his wife Louise from—of all things—chronic liver disease.

David placed his hands on my shoulders and looked me straight in the eye. "They've agreed to take Jane at Chapel Hill."

The only part I heard as I fell to my knees was that they'd agreed to take her. "Thank God," I gasped. "When?"

"They're working on a bed in ICU right now." Dr. Byrd pulled me to my feet. "I expect to be sending her in less than an hour. You've got to go home, pack a bag and get back up here as soon as you can."

The haze around me never lifted. To this day I don't remember Dr. Byrd leaving to go back to Jane. Nor do I remember walking out of the waiting room nor what happened to Jimmy and Patti. Like driving in and out of dense fog-covered roads, my life just came and went. It was as if I had been placed on automatic pilot. I had to get our two dogs, Thumper and Little Mutt, over to Jane's mother's house. I remember dropping them off and facing her; finally telling her not only what had happened, but about Jane's illness, the severity of which we'd kept hidden from her. Privacy to Jane was something she treasured more than anything; an acute shyness she'd developed at childhood that at times made her appear aloof, even snobbish—a trait that those who knew her were keenly aware never existed.

Later as I stumbled back into the ICU waiting room not knowing when I would be going, only that at some point I'd be leaving for Chapel Hill. Not sure if I'd even packed let alone who I'd called, I found Ron Moore waiting for me. Ron was Jane's primary physician—but he was more than that. Right up there with Jimmy and Patti, he was not just Jane's doctor and mine as well; Ron was one of my closest friends. For more than eighteen years, he and I had raced sailboats together, and many a night had stayed up way past midnight with way too much wine solving the problems of the world. I love this man. His weak smile assured me again the seriousness of what awaited Jane. I am one of the few people he'd ever shown his emotions to and that day I read his face. He looked scared.

"When's she leaving?" I asked as I plopped down in a chair, hungry and exhausted.

Ron shook his head and walked to the window that overlooked the doctors' parking lot at the rear of the hospital. "Come here," he said.

I wearily pushed myself up and walked over to the window. His eyes never met mine as his gaze remained fixed on something outside the window. "They're getting ready to lift off." Ron pointed to the EastCare helicopter sitting on the helipad on the other side of the parking lot; its rotors just beginning to turn. Seconds later, as I stood frozen at the window, I watched as the helicopter started its slow ascent.

Bracing myself against the window, I turned to Ron. "I thought she'd be going by ambulance."

"Look, Skip," Ron's eyes met mine. The faint laugh that always covered his real feelings when he has bad news, conflicted with a single tear that slipped out of the corner of his eye. "David and I both agree that she might not make it in an ambulance. This is her best chance."

My legs gave way as I struggled to find a place to sit. Before I fell, Ron grabbed me and led me to a couch. My aching heart crumbled as Ron sat down beside me. I knew that Jane was critical, and deep inside I'd feared that she might not make it but no one else had suggested that she might die. With both of her doctors concerned that Jane "might not make it," the bleak reality of what was happening to her slapped me in the face like finding out that the world might end tomorrow. As far as I was concerned, if Jane died, I might as well die with her. For without her, it would be the end of the world for me.

"You mean—?" my trembling voice failed to get the words out as tears rolled down my cheeks and into my mouth, filling my throat. Ron nodded as he placed his hands on my shoulders. The strength I'd tried to show all morning, dried up like a rain puddle on a hot summer day. Ron held me as I fell to pieces in his arms.

Chapter
3

*M*Y SISTER Debby is as close to a living angel as there can be. In all my confusion, I had not thought to call Debby that June day when Jane first fell so ill. I've always been close to her, but with my thinking in turmoil, I only remembered to call her when I left the hospital to pack. As I said goodbye to Ron and left the ICU waiting room, I literally bumped into my sister as I wandered down the hall heading for the elevator.

"How is she?" Debby asked, as she reached up and wrapped her arms around me.

Debby is four-feet-eleven and a half inches of pure dynamite; a whirlwind of strength, intelligence and emotion. Her relationship with Jane was more like a sister than a sister-in-law. They loved each other unconditionally.

"She just left for Chapel Hill," I said, holding onto her as if she would disappear if I let go. "I'm right behind her. Walk me to my car and I'll tell you all I can. I don't have much time."

As we traveled down the elevator, through the front doors and into the parking lot, I told my sister as much as I knew. From the time that Jane had been diagnosed some eight months before, she'd kept her illness within the walls of our home, not letting many within that secluded sanctuary. Only one or two of her closest friends knew how sick Jane actually was. Debby was one of the special ones, but like the others, much of Jane's pain and suffering was shared with only me. That was about to change.

As I opened the door to my car and reached to hug Debby goodbye, she stepped back and asked, "Can I go with you?"

"What?" Jane and I had been through so much together and the thought of anyone—including family—going with me to Chapel Hill had never crossed my mind.

"I know how Jane is, but you need someone. I've got a bag packed. Can I go with you?"

"What about Pete and Jenna?" Pete was her husband and Jenna, her ten-year-old daughter.

"I've talked to them both and they want me to be with you."

Like water racing from an unclogged drain, all the pent-up adrenaline rushed from me, leaving me stunned and empty. Afraid and unglued, I fell into my sister's arms and again I lost all control and wept. My tiny little sister felt more like a giant to me as she stood in the parking lot holding me up. This time, my weeping gave way to wails as years of pain flowed down her sleeve. When I finally got control of myself, I wiped my eyes and said, "Yes."

"ONE MORE DAY, one more tide, one more sunset. Baby, I'll be satisfied. But then again, I know what I would do, I'd be wishing, dear, for One More Day with you."[1]

"Turn that up," I said.

"What?" my sister turned, her cell phone still stuck in her ear.

---

[1] *One More Day,* written by Bobby Tomberlin and Steven Dale. Released by Diamond Rio 2000.

"Turn that up," I repeated.

"Hold on," Debby told the caller as she placed her knee under the steering wheel and reached for the radio, all the while never letting the phone slip from here ear. "Skip wants the radio up."

The song, by Diamond Rio, sifted through the interior of Debby's Tahoe as I sat back absorbing every word and phrase. When the song ended, I closed my eyes and prayed. "Oh God, please give me one more day with her," I begged. "Just one more day." But in my heart of hearts, just like in the song, I knew if He granted my wish, I'd thank Him and pray for one more.

The trip to Chapel Hill—a blur of phone calls and moments of desperate quiet—seemed to take forever. For the first time, I brought my closest friends into the fold of privacy that Jane had created. For the first time, it was time for me to call the shots and I needed help. Throughout the ordeal of Jane's illness, our friends had opened their arms trying to reach us. All I could tell them was that if and when the time came, I'd call, hoping and praying that the day would never come. But that day had come—no, it didn't just come, it swept over me like a tidal wave leaving me far from home, bruised, battered, and afraid. During the drive to the hospital, I called out for help and it came in an avalanche of love and kindness. George Bailey said during the final scene of *It's a Wonderful Life* that a man can be judged by the friends who have touched his life. For the first time, that day, I knew what he meant.

I used to say that the best four years of my life had been when I attended UNC at Chapel Hill. My college years were magical and I loved the experience, but the UNC that I remembered was one of fun and learning. The UNC I was about to explore would be one of antiseptic walls, the quiet hush of medical students on rounds, along with the ever-presence of blinking and ticking machines that resembled televisions only that

30

the screen had numbers and graphs instead of pictures. It was late when Debby and I finally reached the hospital.

On weekdays, the UNC Hospitals are a buzz of traffic and people. In fact, there is so much traffic that passes through the covered portico's, that uniformed officers complete with whistles and white gloves direct the cars and pedestrians that flow in and out of the three buildings.

But nights and weekends are a different animal altogether. The absence of cars and people outside is further amplified by the emptiness of the lobbies and halls inside. The main lobby is dominated by a huge work of mobile art that rises two stories into the balcony that houses the cafeteria. Colored balls ping and bounce inside the light blue cage. They ride up chains then spill onto tracks that whir them around in circles where they set windmills and stoppers into action that in turn release other colored balls that ping and bounce over and over in a perpetual motion. During the day, the mobile holds the fascination of many a child. But at night, in that vast lobby, its constant echoing only adds to the loneliness of the empty chamber.

After checking with the only person on duty, we found our way to the intensive care unit. MICU, as it is called, lies inside a pair of operator-controlled doors. To enter, a visitor must pick up an adjacent phone and announce their intentions. Only two people are allowed in during visiting hours. However, the very capable and friendly staff of nurses and doctors always make exceptions and Debby and I were allowed in long enough to see Jane.

I walked to her bed and grabbed her hand, hoping that she would somehow know that I was there with her. Knowing that she'd at least made it to UNC released the fatigue that I'd been ignoring for much of

31

the day. "Bone Tired" may be an overused cliché, but it is the best expression that I can use to describe the exhaustion that crept through my body. Recognizing my weariness, Debby touched me gently on my shoulder. "We need to go," she said.

"I can't." I gripped Jane's hand tighter.

"You're beat." Debby turned me so that she could look at my face. "I can see it in your eyes."

"I can't." I said again turning back to Jane.

"Skip, she made it here. She's in good hands. God brought her this far for a reason. Trust Him. He's doing His part and tomorrow you've got to do yours. You've got to have a clear head."

I nodded. I knew she was right. Reluctantly, I leaned over, kissed Jane and slowly let go of her hand.

As I left her room, I prayed in my heart, "Oh God, please, one more day. Oh please, just give me *one more day.*"

Chapter
4

*O*N BOARD THE SHUTTLE that would take Debby and me to the hospital, I wiped my eyes trying to awaken from the sleep that came too quickly the night before. We'd checked into the local Holiday Inn when we left the hospital and after a couple of glasses of wine and a few more phone calls, I slipped into a dreamless sleep. Even though I'd now been awake for more than an hour, the emotional battle still raged inside me and I felt as if I'd been run over by a bulldozer. As we made our way to the hospital, I stared blankly out the window while my sister made small talk with the other passengers. "What are ya'll up here for?" Debby asked the women sitting in front of her.

"My sister is on the list for a liver transplant," the woman answered.

Slowly I turned my head and cocked it to one side. "What did you say?"

The woman placed her hand on the shoulder of the person sitting beside her. "My name is Betty Smith and this is my sister Wilma. She's the one on the list. We're here for her six-month check-up. What brings you two to Chapel Hill?"

"My sister-in-law is here," my sister took over, answering quickly. "We're praying to get her on the list, too, but we may be too late. She's mighty sick. I'm so

33

afraid that she won't make the list before she needs a liver and that they will send her home to die."

For much of my life I'd viewed chance meetings as just random acts of fate, more akin to a gambler rolling a seven the first time out. There was a time that I might have bought that assumption, but not any more. I believe that chance meetings are anything but. Sometimes I think that those meetings were planned long before we ever take our first breath. No, chance had nothing to do with the fact that those two women shared the van with us that morning. It was a way for God to speak to my sister and me.

"That will never happen," Betty said.

"What?" Debby and I said at the same time.

"Trust me," Wilma interrupted. "They won't do that. I don't know how they do it, but they'll find her a liver, one way or another. They will never send her home to die."

I swallowed hard and looked at Debby. Before I could speak, she asked. "Are you sure?"

"I've been close to death on two occasions," Wilma looked over at me with a reassuring smile, "before I ever made the list. Somehow they brought me back both times. But both times there were plans to not only put me on the list, but to put me at the top."

Could it really be true? I'd never heard that and the doubter in me found it hard to believe. Most of the doctors I'd met at UNC seemed cordial and compassionate—just like the doctors at home. But not those on the liver transplant team. Headed by a four-foot-ten-inch Canadian by the name of Steven Zacks, a man with the personality of a four-cylinder Mustang, they guarded the livers as if they would be giving up their own. I wished—no—I prayed that the woman was right, but deep inside, something told me that she was wrong.

The van pulled up to the main entrance and the driver got out and opened the side door. As the women stepped out, Betty leaned back into the van and looked at me. "What's your wife's name?"

"Jane," I said.

"I'll be praying for her," she said as she turned and walked toward the automatic doors.

"Tell Wilma we'll be praying for her, too," I called back as she disappeared into the cavernous lobby.

THROUGHOUT MY LIFE, I felt as if I could fix anything. When Jane dented the car, I always got it fixed. If I chipped a tooth, I'd get it fixed. Jane breaks a leg, I take care of things. Deep down inside I knew I couldn't fix Jane. But one thing I did know was that unless she got on that transplant list, they couldn't fix her either. I was determined that if I never did anything else for the rest of my life, I was going to get her on that list.

I've danced in and out of politics most of my life starting with my college major and right on up to supporting the right elected people from the school board to the governor's office. In all those years, I'd never called in a marker. I'd never asked to be placed on a board nor had I ever asked for any favors. That was about to change.

Fortunately, one of Jane's best friends was the North Carolina Lt. Governor, Beverly Perdue. That friendship had been forged long before Beverly had entered politics, and even though Jane was Republican and Beverly was a Democrat, that had never been a subject of discussion between the two of them. They loved each other. And it came as no surprise when the first person to visit the Intensive Care Unit was Beverly. Beverly is one of the kindest and most compassionate people I have ever known. She is also as genuine as it gets, but a part of me still smiles when I recall the day she

35

walked into the ICU. The sign outside states that before one can enter, they must announce their intentions via the phone and turn off their cell phones. When Beverly enters a room, it is an experience. And that day at the ICU was no exception. I can still see the faces on the nurses as Beverly Perdue, swept unannounced through the double doors, waving and telling each person she passed that she was there to see Jane Crayton, all the while talking on her cell. Whether she meant to do it or not, I'll never know. But I can assure you that it probably took less than an hour for the word to spread throughout the hospital that Jane Crayton had a very special friend.

Chapter
5

*T*HE DAYS IN THE ICU slowly melted one into the other as Jane lay unconscious, plugged into an array of machines, each one beeping and broadcasting to a central station where a cadre of nurses monitored each setting. I'd made it clear to every person who worked in the unit—doctors, nurses and technicians—that as long as Jane occupied space at UNC, I would be at her side. "Until she gets a liver," I told them, "if you want to find me, I'd be in her room or asleep at the Holiday Inn." It also didn't take long for the word to spread where my commitment was.

Watching someone while a machine breathes for them is painful, but when that person is someone you love, it is excruciating. I remember when my father died. After a failed operation, against his wishes, he had been placed in the ICU on a ventilator to keep him alive. I can vividly remember his pleading eyes, demanding that he be unhooked. Only when my mother, in the bravest thing she'd ever done, told the doctors to remove the tube, did he eventually pass on in peace.

The case with Jane was just the opposite. Although we'd both talked about the consequences of extending life, the machine that was breathing for her was there to keep her alive so that she could come back to me. I just didn't believe that God was ready for her yet. One day I would soon find out that not only was He not

37

ready for her yet as she slept in almost suspended animation, He was speaking to her.

I've been told that people in a coma can actually hear and feel one's presence. No one has ever confirmed that to me, so Debby and I took no chances. Each day we took turns talking to Jane. We talked about everything—recalled old memories, gossiped, and even read aloud. Sometimes we'd just sit by Jane's bed and hold her hand. As the days crawled by, we began to see small bits of improvement, not so much in giant steps, but more like baby steps. Then, after about three days, Jane began to breathe on her own. For the first time in almost a week, I began to breathe again as well. I thought I could see a tiny light at the end of the tunnel. I just prayed that it was a glimpse of daylight and not the headlight of an oncoming train. Two days later, on June 7th, Jane was alert enough to be moved to a private room. Debby and I fell to our knees and thanked God.

The next morning, I awakened early and caught the shuttle to the hospital. I wanted to be with Jane as soon as I could. It was Saturday, June 8th; our anniversary. Thirty-four years earlier I had met her at the chancel rail at Centenary Methodist Church in downtown New Bern and pledged to love her forever. More than any other time we'd been together, I wanted to spend that morning with her and re-pledge those vows to her.

Like the weekend before, the hospital seemed almost deserted as I walked across the inlaid terrazzo that covered the vast entry. The click of my heels echoed from the floor and bounced off the huge plate glass windows, competing with the constant pinging of the giant perpetual motion machine. The only other living thing in the room was a uniformed clerk snoozing at the information desk. As I walked past her, she never lifted her head.

I found a flower machine just to the right of the elevator, placed my money into the bill grabber and made my selection. Jane's favorite flower had always been red roses. During the fall of our senior year in high school, she had been dating another guy. At the time, we were—you might say—best friends. But I wanted more. So in an effort to try and win her favor, for her eighteenth birthday, I sent her a dozen long-stemmed red roses. I know beyond any doubt that that bouquet won her heart for me. The other guy disappeared forever.

The day before, when we left, Jane was alert, yet still in somewhat of a confused state. Debby and I were assured that the confusion was a leftover from the encephalopathy coma and that eventually she would come around. We were told to not worry if she didn't rebound right away, that within a few days she would come back to us fully.

As I walked into her room, Jane was sitting up in bed. Her arms had been tied to the side to keep her from removing her feeding tube. Immediately, she started to cry when she saw me and the roses.

"So you like the roses," I said as I leaned over and kissed away her tears.

"Uh huh," she answered.

"Do you remember the first time I gave you roses?" I asked, placing the flowers in the window by her bed.

"No," she answered in a childlike voice.

I turned back to her. "It was on your eighteenth birthday. Now do you remember?"

"Uh huh." She answered.

"Do you know what day it is?" I sat on the edge of the bed and reached for her hand.

"No. I've been sick, I think," the child in her spoke again.

"It's June 8th," I said. "Our anniversary."

Jane's eyes welled up and again she cried. "Oh no. I forgot. I can't seem to remember anything."

"Do you know who I am?" I asked.

Jane whimpered through her tears, "You're Skip. I love you."

At first I thought the roses had triggered the emotion. It was only when I realized that, in her confused state, she was clueless as to the date, and it was me she was so happy to see. I knelt down beside her bed and we wept together.

Chapter 6

*N*OW, GETTING JANE ON THE LIST for a liver became the most important thing in my life. For most people, getting on the list is a long and arduous journey, sometimes taking years to accomplish. I couldn't count on what the ladies in the van had said that day. After what had happened to Jane, we could not wait. She had to be listed for her to live. For maybe the first time in my life, I had a firm grip on what I needed to do. Whatever it took, I had to make sure that she'd be on that list.

There are "Ah-ha" moments at some point in all our lives, and I was approaching one of those times. Before that moment, I had been accustomed to taking whatever life had to dish out to me and rolling with the punches. As much as I had been a fixer, I had been taught that there were times when one had to make the best of things. I had always been one who played by the rules; waiting in line for my turn. Authorities were to be respected. Isn't that what a good southern boy learned in kindergarten?

When our daughter Mary Ruth was born, she struggled every day for a week trying to be a part of our lives. It was through that instant and unconditional love for her that I learned what being a father was all about. I prayed daily that God would take me and let her live. And my love for Jane was just as strong and

41

unconditional. I would have surely given my life for Jane at that moment. She could have had my liver, but I am A-positive and she was O-negative. The irony of life is that O-negative is the universal donor and I could have taken Jane's liver, but she could only take one that was O-negative. I had to do something, but there had to be something more than just standing in line and praying. Her only chance to live was in the hands of a team of doctors who would decide her fate. I had to make sure that the decision would be made in our favor and I was willing to do anything to make it happen.

And I had a partner: Jane and her attitude, and desire to live became the real source of what was to come.

Organs are precious commodities and those who provide them know how precious they are. It's not just about the donors, yet without them there would be no organs. It is also about the team of specialists who are placed in the position to make sure that those special gifts are not given in vain.

Because of that, transplant teams are made up of many specialists. In Jane's case, the team included a surgeon, a radiologist, a gastroenterologist, a cardiologist, and a psychologist. Even a social worker was attached to the team and, of course, her liver doctor. Each team member had a special part in the selection of who got a liver. The patient would have to pass each test to make sure that they are healthy enough to live with the new organ, so as not to waste the transplant. Again, with Jane, they would not give her a liver if she had heart problems or any form of cancer, or any other health problem that might become terminal. Livers are hard to come by, and the selection process, as it applies to the recipient's physical and mental health, is paramount.

The team is headed by the liver doctor, who makes the live-or-die decision. It would be Dr. Zacks—that short Napoleonic-looking man who would eventually have the final say. Although he was lacking in the area of personal relationships, it was obvious to me that this man was brilliant. I would later find that beyond that professional exterior, the man had a heart. Yet, for now, his personality didn't matter to me. I wanted brains.

Jane and I spent our anniversary together that Saturday with her mostly in a confused state-of-mind. At times I found her to be coherent. Other times she cried. But it was her child-like quality that baffled me. It was something that I could not figure out. That day, sitting in the quiet of her hospital room something dawned on me. It was as if I had been struck by lightning. I realized that the person lying in the bed next to me was not the same person I'd known for more than forty years. Something had changed—a change so dramatic that it would come to touch more lives than she had ever known, a change that would be a part of her for the rest of her life.

Chapter 7

*T*HROUGHOUT MY LIFE I've often heard when things happened that are beyond our comprehension, that "God moves in *mysterious* ways." That may be consoling to some, but I like to think that it is more like that "God moves in *determined* ways." If we really sit back and ponder what happens in our lives, sooner or later we realize that God is a part of every single phase, from our birth to our death. I believe that He has a plan for each of us, but along with that plan, He gives us free will. It is through that gift that we often choose to deviate from God's will. The more we move away from what He has planned, the more determined God becomes to bring us back. Sometimes He places road blocks in our way and sometimes they are as simple as a thought or an epiphany. Eventually, some of us get it. But there are many who just don't. One thing, however, is for sure: God never stops trying.

As the days slowly moved ahead and Jane became more coherent, I realized that her childlike behavior was not just a byproduct of the encephalopathy. I noticed a real change in the way she looked at life and the way she accepted people. There was a glow about her and the doctors and nurses saw it too. They loved attending to her and visiting with her. One wonderful nurse found Jane so captivating that she came in on her day off just to wash Jane's hair. Jane began to develop a sense of humor I'd never seen before and she loved sharing it with others.

I first noticed it as she begged to be taken off the feeding tube. She wanted something real to eat; she was hungry. But instead of complaining or crying when the doctors said no, she acted more like a little girl. She would say things like "Can I have a cookie?" or "I would really love a banana, would you go get me a banana?" One day as I dozed in the chair next to her bed, I noticed a stranger standing in the door. When I cleared my head I heard, "Mister, you look like a nice man, would you get me a cookie?" She'd snared the guy as he'd walked by her door.

As the tests continued to pave the way for Jane's acceptance on the transplant list, just as the doctors had said, each day Jane got a little better and became more aware of her surroundings. Finally, they let her eat. I'll never forget what she asked for. She told me to go down to the snack bar and bring her a cookie and a banana. While she grew stronger, the change in Jane became more animated, and yet the little girl in her would not go away. With all she'd been through, for the first time in our life together, I could tell that she was truly happy. Something had happened to her during those six days in ICU. The things that had been so important to Jane in the past did not matter to her anymore. Family and friends would now take a front seat in her life and her driver would be God, someone we'd not spent a lot of time with in the past several years.

One day, as Debby and I sat in Jane's room awaiting her return from the final test, there seemed to be an air of excitement in the hall. Nurses and doctors fussed with the room, an orderly came in and quickly changed the sheets on Jane's bed. Shortly after, a distinguished-looking man in a long white coat appeared at the door, followed by an entourage of staffers. As he approached me, he held out his hand and said, "Mr. Crayton, I'm Dr. Jeffrey Houpt, dean of the medical school. I wanted to meet Jane and to speak to you both."

"This is really an honor," I said. "But I'm afraid Jane is not here, she's somewhere having another test."

Before Dr. Houpt could answer, the crowd of onlookers behind him parted like the Red Sea. As Jane entered the room, she was being pushed, not by an orderly, but by Dr. Doug Morgan, an affable young man who was the gastro guy on the Transplant team. *What an impression Jane had made on everyone in this hospital,* I thought.

"I'm Jane," she said. "Poop doctor," the name she called Dr. Morgan, "has just been poking around in my butt which, by the way, might have been a lot of fun for him, but was no picnic for me. Whew, I'm glad that's over."

"Jane, I've heard so much about you," Dr. Houpt said as he shook her hand. "I've been told that you gave us all a pretty good scare, but I understand you're on the mend. I just wanted to see you before you were discharged."

"Dr. Houpt," I interrupted. "What do you mean discharged?"

He looked at Jane and picked up her hand. "Jane, are you ready to go home?"

"Oh my God yes," she replied. "And sleep in my own bed?"

"I think that's the plan. Dr. Morgan says that we've done all we can do for you here in Chapel Hill and he's going to send you back to Dr. Byrd."

Jane turned to look at Dr. Morgan. "Poop doctor, you mean I can go home today?"

"As soon as I can get a transfer person up here, you can go home." Dr. Morgan said, smiling.

"Wait a minute," I objected. "She's not going anyplace. Not until she gets on that list."

Dr. Houpt smiled and looked at Dr. Morgan. "You tell him."

"Mr. Crayton, I don't think I can ever remember a more dedicated family than you and your sister have been to Jane. This morning, the liver transplant team met and Jane has been placed on the list. You'll be getting a formal letter on Tuesday."

Tears welled up in my eyes, then streamed down my cheeks. Like that first day at Craven Regional, my knees began to buckle. My sister tried to steady me as we both fell to our knees. "Thank God," I cried. "Thank God."

When I regained my composure, I hugged and thanked everyone in the room, even the janitor. As Dr. Houpt started to leave, he turned to Jane and asked, "Is there anything I can do for you."

"Yes, there is," she said.

"And what is that?"

Jane smiled, a twinkle in her eye, "Can I have a cookie?"

THE ELEVEN DAYS at Chapel Hill ended almost as abruptly as they'd started. One minute we were praying for a chance for Jane to be listed, and the next we were in Debby's Tahoe headed east. A miracle had surely occurred. Before, Jane had hidden her illness like a malady. Now it was as if a switch had been thrown. She would never again hide in the shadows of her illness. Her disease and how it affected her was now an open book. The trip home was a blur of phone calls to and from loved ones with frequent stops for ice cream. The internet was abuzz with news that Jane was coming home.

As we journeyed home, the afternoon sun danced between the trees and houses that lined Highway 70. How different things were, I thought, from that gloomy

47

Sunday afternoon my sister and I traveled to Chapel Hill. If the sun had shown that day, I had not noticed. Eleven days—a span that would have flashed by almost unnoticed in what used to be my normal mundane existence. Yet, to me, those days seemed like a lifetime. A lifetime? Sure. But even more, a life-changing time. Whatever it was that Jane saw while in that coma, it had changed her forever.

But the very fact of all that had happened changed me as well. Those eleven days brought to me, in no uncertain terms, a taste of the reality of life. I now knew what really mattered. But more than just knowing what did and did not matter, now I could tell the difference.

When we finally arrived home, a smiling Jimmy and Patti waited for us on the deck. Inside, Jane's mom and our two dogs Thumper and Little Mutt couldn't wait to jump all over her. The reunion that I'd prayed for had finally come. As I stood in line for my share of the hugs, I thanked God for bringing my girl home. She was not well, not by a long shot, but now there was a chance. For the first time in almost two years, there was hope. I thought that just maybe we'd be able to fulfill one of the vows we'd made to each other on our wedding day and grow old together. God had given me "One more day."

Chapter
8

*E*NCEPHALOPATHY is controlled by a drug called Lactulose. It is an ultra-sweet drink that looks and smells a lot like honey. It is taken orally and its basic function is to flush the bowel system to prevent the build up of ammonia in the small intestines. It is the ammonia that triggers the confused state called encephalopathy, which in its worst case— like what happened to Jane—sends the patient into a coma.

In order to prevent a bout with it, patients must drink a couple of ounces of the medicine every three to four hours round the clock. From time to time, occasionally without warning, the patient slips into a confused state requiring that a dose be given every hour on the hour for twenty to thirty hours before the patient comes around.

In most cases with Jane, there would be some sort of warning, generally something simple like forgetting where something was stored or a special friend's name. In time I learned to pick up on those signals and would quickly increase the frequency of doses, which would circumvent the episode either completely or at least moderate it.

A week after we'd come back home, I missed a signal. I was helping Jane set the dining-room table when she asked if we had a leaf to expand it from eight people to

49

ten. When I reminded her that we had one in the hall closet, she shook it off with a shrug and laughed.

"Of course," she said. "How silly of me. I knew that." Before dinner, she had lapsed back into one of her episodes.

She could not tell me her birth date or her mother's maiden name. When I held up three fingers, she saw one. When I held up one, she saw four. This time, however, I knew what to do. The doctors at Chapel Hill had told me that if caught in time, a coma could easily be circumvented. The minute I recognized her slipping back, I started her on increased doses of Lactulose. Yet unlike before, she did not reject her medicine. For all purposes, she was out of it, except this time she took her medicine without protest. It was as if deep down inside, she knew that an hourly dose of Lactulose was her only way back to reality.

When someone you love slips outside of reality, it is a scary thing. The level to where Jane had slipped was somewhere between what is real and what is make-believe. She knew where she was and she knew me. Everything else was a fantasy to her and to her, it all made sense. But for me it was as if she had joined John and Wendy and flown to Never-Never Land. To me, nothing she said made sense at all.

We take verbal communication so much for granted. When conversation between someone we know and love takes a vacation, it is hugely frustrating. If I was to bring Jane back into my reality, my job was clear. I had to give her the medicine every hour on the hour, which meant I had to be up with her all night, a task I was more than willing to do.

By morning, she had been drinking her medicine for approximately eighteen hours. Throughout the night, she had been a model patient. Not once did she give me a bit of trouble nor did she reject the doses. Usually she'd wake up, take a swig and fall back fast asleep. It

50

didn't take long before I was able to follow the same routine. I don't know if it was fear or fatigue or both, but she was not coming around and I had been cautioned not to increase the dosage more than once an hour. So I called Dr. Byrd's office and left a message with his service. Dr. Byrd got back with me immediately and instructed me to get Jane to the emergency room. Even with all the assurances given to me by the doctors at UNC, my life began to replay in front of me. My hands shook as I wiped the sweat from my palms. I called our friend Annie Parker and told her what was going on. She assured me that she would be over right away and hung up without saying goodbye.

Annie and Larry Parker moved to New Bern from Indiana in the mid-seventies when Larry took a position as an OB/GYN doctor in one of the local firms. They bought a house near us and immediately we built a wonderful friendship. Next to Patti Jones, Annie became one of Jane's very best friends. Her quirky sense of humor has always kept us in stenches when we're together. Annie was also an RN and I knew she'd know what to do.

When I returned to our bedroom to try to prepare Jane for the trip to the hospital, I found her in the bathroom sitting on the john. What I was about to learn was that the lactulose was beginning to work. By the time Annie got to the house, Jane had recovered most of her senses. By the time we reached the emergency room, she'd rejoined the living. I could not believe the transformation.

Just to make sure, Dr. Byrd admitted Jane to the hospital for observation. Late the next day, he released her and within an hour we'd picked up her mother and were on our way to our family cottage at Atlantic Beach to spend the 4th of July Holiday week.

Over time, I got pretty good at picking up the little signals that would indicate a slip backward and could, by increasing her dosage, avoid an episode. But as much as I tried to catch those little hints, from time to time I'd miss one and Jane would find herself back visiting Tinkerbelle and Peter. The good news was that on the rare occasions that a relapse occurred, within twenty-four hours, I could bring her back without a visit to the hospital or call to the doctor. The best news was that, as time moved forward, the episodes grew further apart.

Chapter 9

UR LIFE TOGETHER settled into what we called normalcy. To others, normalcy might have been day-to-day routines; working, coming home to kids and TV, shopping, marketing, visiting with friends and family, and church on Sundays. For Jane and me, life became less mundane. Family and friends became more important. Lingering after a sunset, basting in its warmth and brilliance overruled the local news on the TV. And walking on the beach. For most of our time together, Atlantic Beach had not just played a part in our life, it had been a part of our life together. From our first kiss to our last, that stretch of sand held more memories for us than any other place in the world. Even in the winter, the magic continued.

We began to look at life through a different lens. Life for us had gone from mere existence to actually living each day as if it were our last. Life had moved from the repetitive to an adventure. To us, tomorrow was no longer assured; it was only a promissory note. Retirement and the future was something we could not count on, even as Jane got better. Jane's illness had changed us both. Life was to be lived in the present. An "I love you" was not to be saved until later; it was to be spoken in the moment.

There was one thing missing in our lives. Jane and I were both Christians, but we did not attend church regularly. In fact, in the ten years preceding her illness, we'd spent very little time inside a church. We'd been baptized and later married in Centenary United Methodist Church in downtown New Bern. During our early years of marriage, we'd been very active at Centenary with me teaching Sunday School and Jane involved in youth activities. For one reason or another we'd drifted away from the church. There may have been outside circumstances that contributed to our leaving the fold. During our thirties, we became very active in racing sailboats, which I'm sure had something to do with our departure. I have also blamed it on the roller coaster assignments of pastors, common for years in the church. As soon as the bishop would send a really great leader to serve a church, four or five years later, he'd move him and replace that person with a "dud." I had seen the church grow under the leadership of some really great preachers only to watch its decline following the appointment of someone not so great.

I don't know whether it was that roller coaster ride of great-verses-mediocre church leadership, or the lure of winning sailboat races on Sundays that pulled me away from the church, but Jane and I did not attend much at all. We were Christians, and still members of Centenary, but we just didn't go to church. That was all about to change.

During our active years at Centenary, we were blessed with several outstanding pastors. The one who married Jane and me, the one who helped us deal with the death of our daughter Mary Ruth, and one who, along with his wife, became lifelong friends. Preachers are usually held in awe by most parishioners, so it is a special gift when a friendship develops that allows them to let their hair down and be themselves. Even preachers need best friends and confidants.

But of all the pastors who have touched my life, none has done so like Powell Osteen—a more Christ-like man, I've never known. If the sun rising in the east is an indisputable fact, that Jane was touched by the hand of God while in that coma is also one. We needed a church. There are places that have a feel about them. It's like when you know the moment is right; like meeting your soul mate or looking into the eyes of your child for the first time. There is something about the moment that you "know" is right. That's how Jane and I felt the first time we attended Garber United Methodist Church. We felt like we'd come home.

I realize that a pastor does not make a church and that the feelings Jane and I experienced that day were about the family of God and not just Pastor Powell, but it was his guidance that was the pulse of the congregation. Powell is one of the hardest working men I know. The day for this six-foot-five, grey-headed teddy bear of a man starts before sunrise and ends well after dark. How he is able to teach a men's Bible Study Class, mentor a couples Disciple Class, council engaged couples as well as those having marital problems, visit the sick, host missions, prepare a sermon, run the day-to-day operations of a church, and still find time to spend with his family, is beyond me. And yet, what amazes me most is that he truly loves and cares about each and every member of his flock, and they all know it.

Once we found Garber, Sunday mornings were not enough. Ecclesia, a weeknight service that varied from lectures to studies on how to be a better parent or spouse, to courses comparing the teachings of Sigmund Freud to those of C.S Lewis, became a regular part of our Wednesday nights. Jane started studying the Bible, first on her own, then as a part of a weekly Tuesday morning study group. To say that we had become Jesus Freaks would have been a gross over statement. For me, it was the fulfillment that I had finally reconnected with the spiritual part of my life. For Jane, it would become more, much, much more. Her reconnection would—in a short time—touch more lives than either of us would ever comprehend.

Chapter
10

*O*THER THAN MONTHLY CHECKUPS here in New Bern and bi-yearly checkups in Chapel Hill, there were several other requirements that Jane had to adhere to while she was on the transplant list. One was to always have a bag packed and to carry a pager at all times. Notice of an organ could come at any time and the transplant team had to be able to contact Jane immediately. She had to be ready to leave at a moments notice.

For months, Jane and I stood by praying for the beeper to go off, ready to head back to Chapel Hill and receive the gift of life that someone else—a perfect stranger—had died to provide. From time to time, we'd be startled when the pager went off only to find out when we called the hospital that the page was just a part of the monthly testing the team did to make sure the beeper was working. When the call finally came, it was from a most unusual source.

The liver transplant list is not set up on a first-come-first-serve basis. It is a number based on need and survivability of risk. The number is known as a MELD Score, which stands for Model for End-stage Liver Disease and is derived by a computation of the patience's INR, billirubin and creatinine variables. The higher the number, the more likely a patient will be called. The United Network for Organ Sharing, or UNOS, is the organization responsible for allocating livers for transplants. They use a numbering system for that allocation, hence the MELD Score. Anything above a 40 usually indicates impending death. A number 10 or less generally means that the transplant operation itself would be more risky than the 4% chance of mortality associated with the lower number. Those with 10 or less are generally never called.

Jane's number at the time was 24, which meant that there was a 76% chance that without a transplant she would die. Once a patient is selected by the hospital's transplant team, the livers are provided by an *Organ Procurement Organization* or OPO, a nonprofit organization whose main purpose is to place donor organs with recipients. In North Carolina, that process is handled by *Carolina Donor Services*. One Friday morning in the fall of 2002, I received a call on my cell phone. The person on the other end identified herself as a nurse with *Carolina Donor Services*.

When I asked her why she'd called, she said, "Mr. Crayton, someone has died and left your wife a liver. Do you want it?"

Stunned by what I'd just heard, it felt like the air in my car had suddenly been sucked out as I blindly slid through an intersection, running a red light. Slamming on the brakes, I brought my car to a stop on the shoulder of the road.

"What did you just say?" I asked, my hand shaking as I shifted into park.

"Do you know a Mike Rowe?" the caller asked.

"Sure, he's my nephew's father-in-law. But what's he got to do with all this?" I asked in rapid fire staccato.

"He died last night and left his organs to specific people and he wanted your wife to have his liver," the nurse informed me.

"Is that legal? How? Why? When?" The words came without sentences as I tried to make sense of it all.

"Yes, Mr. Crayton," the nurse said. "Here, let me explain."

Jane's sister Ann died at the age of thirty-two. Her death was the most traumatic event to affect Jane in her entire life. Even the passing of her mother and father did not dig as deeply into her soul as the death of her sister. As Jane grew up, Ann had become her surrogate mother, so her loss went far deeper than the loss of a sister. Some years later, a wonderful therapist would help Jane to uncover the pain Ann's passing had caused and to eventually let it go.

When Ann died, she left an eleven-year-old girl named Debbie and a four-year-old son named Glenn. Without any children in our lives, they became the closest thing we had to our own kids. As they grew up, we became a part of their lives from attending Cub Scout meetings to football games, from 4-H shows to Junior Miss contests. From birthdays to the day they both got married, we were there every step of the way,

Mike Rowe was Jane's nephew Glenn's father-in-law. The nurse explained to me that Mike had been in a hospital in nearby Raleigh for an operation to repair an aneurism. Although the operation was expected to be routine, the night before, Mike had decided that just in case he did not make it, he not only wanted to give his organs, he wanted to designate who got most of them. Mike knew all too well about Jane's situation and he had elected to give her his liver should the unexpected occur. He had done the same thing with his heart and kidneys. Because of Mike Rowe's generosity and love for others, people are alive today. He will always be a hero to me.

When the nurse had finished, she asked me if I had any questions. And of course I did, hundreds of them. My first question was why I'd heard from her rather than someone from the transplant team at UNC, which was the way I'd been told things would happen. I found out that normally that would be the way things would have happened. However, when a person is designated to receive a bequeathed organ, it worked differently. It was the donor service's responsibility to first contact someone in the recipients family to make sure that the organ was desired. She also warned me that there was more to be done. The availability of a liver was just the first part. It would be up to the transplant team to make sure that Mike's liver would be a match. That we had a liver was a giant leap, but it was not a done deal yet.

Before she hung up, the nurse asked me if I had any more questions. I told her that I did not, but I felt sure that Jane would. She gave me her phone number and told me to call back any time and she'd be happy to answer any other questions that we might have.

"I'm going to call the transplant coordinator at Chapel Hill," she said. "I'm sure you'll hear from her shortly. The rest will be up to them."

When she hung up, I sat in my car on the side of the road trembling. Moments later, I regained as much composure as I could and called Jane.

Chapter
11

AN AFFABLE WOMAN by the name of Kim was the transplant coordinator for the UNC Liver Transplant Team. She was the first person we'd met with the team and the one who'd worked so well with Dr. Byrd arranging the transfer to Chapel Hill when Jane was in the coma. She is a nurse with a master's degree and in many ways Dr. Zack's alter ego. If his personality resembles a four-cylinder Mustang, hers was more like a full size Chevy—large, warm and comfortable. She played the good cop to his bad cop; a toucher who was never far from a comforting hug or a soft compassionate look or remark.

When she called that day, she appeared to be different. Not just more business-like, but almost distant. Kim's first question was the same one the donor service's nurse had asked. "Do you want the liver?"

And again I said, "Yes." Kim informed me that there had to be a series of tests to make sure the liver would match. The most important thing would be the blood type. Kim reminded me that Jane's blood type, O-negative, was extremely rare and that although her blood type made her a universal donor, she could only accept O-negative blood and that the donor's type, namely Mike's, had to match with Jane's for the liver to work. Beyond that, there would be additional tests. But the blood type would be the key issue. Kim warned me not to get my hopes up.

There was one more thing that her voice revealed. I've always been pretty good at reading people, at least when they are lying or hiding something. For those who are not compulsive liars, most have trouble hiding the truth—especially when they are confronted with having to think on their feet. Generally, there is a hesitation in their voices. That day, Kim hesitated several times and that little voice that lives inside me told me that the transplant team did not want to give Mike's liver to Jane. I've often wondered if Kim was being the "front man" and having to answer questions for which she was not prepared. Whatever the case, I don't think there was any malice intended. I just think that Mike's liver became available before the team felt that Jane was ready. In fact, I wondered if the team felt that Jane might not ever need to have a transplant—something that at the time they were not ready to tell either of us.

Later that day, Kim called back. She told me that everything, including Mike's blood, had been a perfect match. Everything but one thing. Mike weighed in at close to four hundred pounds and Jane was just over one hundred ten pounds. Mike's liver was too big to fit in Jane's small cavity.

Jane nor I had gotten our hopes up too high. Something told me that this was a long shot, whether I caught it in Kim's voice or in the back of my mind. Instead of being hugely disappointed, we were both thankful for the opportunity. We had come to terms with the fact that we could both finally let go and let God. It was then and there that I realized that Jane and I could accept God's will and never question Him.

As for Mike Rowe, I'm sure he's in Heaven with God. Because of him, others live. What a gift this special man gave.

Chapter
12

*S*EVERAL YEARS before Jane got sick, she got interested in crafts. That interest led her from painted pillows to painted pots and finally to painted mailboxes. I had spent some years painting watercolors. However, Jane had never shown an interest in anything creative other than cooking. As her interest in crafts grew, so did her interest in painting. At first her work appeared simplistic—almost as if a child had done it. However, as time passed, she became better and better. Soon, this self-taught painter had developed into quite an artist. She placed her wares in consignment shops throughout the east.

One day I asked her which product she produced seemed to be the most popular. She immediately told me that most of her stuff carried a long shelf life, but she couldn't keep the mailboxes in stock. One day I asked her how many mailboxes she could paint in a day. Her response was, "As many as I can sell."

"Could you paint ten a day?" I asked.

"No," she responded. "But I could paint six. Anyway, I don't need to paint anymore than six or eight a month, that's all I can sell."

"But what if you could sell six a day," I asked. "That would be three hundred dollars a day. Could you do it?"

"Of course I could, with one hand tied behind me." Jane cocked her head to one side and gave me a puzzled puppy-dog look. "But I just told you I don't need to paint that many a day."

"What if we could set up an internet site," I suggested. "Then you could sell your mailboxes all over the country."

Jane laughed, "You set that up and I'll paint the mailboxes."

With that challenge, *TheMailboxLady.com* was born. In the early days of the internet, there were two very important things that had to take place if a company was to be successful. One was obtaining the rights to a name that identified your company, and the other was to be listed in the first two or three pages of a search engine. The name of Jane's company was *The Mailbox Lady.* We applied for www.themailboxlady.com and found that it was available. We also found that there were very few people online offering "hand-painted mailboxes" or "decorative mailboxes." In fact, we found that there were very few people even selling mailboxes on the internet. As soon as the site was up, her business took off like a greyhound chasing a rabbit.

In the months after Jane's ordeal at Chapel Hill, there were two things that gave her real peace. One was her insatiable drive to study the Bible and the other was the time she spent in her studio, listening to music and painting mailboxes. Her personal and group study led her to interaction with others seeking the same thing and her time making personalized mailboxes for many people she'd never meet was special. Instead of retreating inward, Jane was reaching out to life and taking me along for the ride.

I found solace in my writing. During much of Jane's time in ICU, writing was a way to escape, even if just for a few minutes. For several years, I had been writing a column for two local newspapers. First, for a monthly directed at the community of Trent Woods called *The Trent Woods Times.* In time, I graduated to writing for

The Sun Journal, a daily with a circulation of around 35,000. When I started writing for *The Sun Journal,* I started getting calls and emails responding to what I'd written. It seemed my columns appealed to people of all ages and all walks of life. Jane got a kick out of the emails and letters I'd get when one of my columns had touched a heart or struck a particular nerve. Often, she'd ask me why I didn't try to put the columns together in book form. As a writer, I knew that finding an agent or publisher would be almost impossible, but Jane would not take no for an answer.

One day she came into my office and made the announcement that she was forming a publishing company. That was the day that *McBryde Publishing* was born. McBryde, Jane's middle name, published my first book, *Remember When.* After Jane's death, I partnered with Bill Benners and MyBryde Publishing began to grow. Since its inception, it has published sixteen books to date: *In this Small Place, New Bern History 101,* and *Historic Images of Havelock and Cherry Point* by Eddie Ellis; *The Truth about Parenting* by Elizabeth Weidle; *My Sister's Keeper* by Bill Benners; *Sunday's Child, My King the President, Hitler's Judas, Sons of Their Fathers, Fifty Years to Midnight, Short Tales and Tall,* and *Zena's Law* by Tom Lewis, *Sweet Dreams and Flying Machines* and *Child's Play* by Debbie Wallis; and my books, *Remember When* and *The Letter Sweater.* There are more on the way.

For us both, dreams were something to experience not something to be put on hold. Jane was really living outside the box, but what happened with her next was far beyond anything I could have ever dreamed.

Chapter
13

*T*HE MAIN BALLROOM at the Sheraton Hotel and Marina in downtown New Bern buzzed with excitement. The room had been filled to capacity. In fact, the original meeting had been scheduled for New Bern Golf and Country Club, but because the members had heard who the keynote speaker would be, it had been moved to the larger facility.

Jane Crayton had been a shy child. Her shyness followed her into womanhood. Even as she matured, Jane found it difficult to be in groups of more than five or six people. At cocktail parties, if she left my side for a one-on-one conversation, she generally kept me in sight so that she could retreat back to me if at anytime her confidence felt threatened.

"Surprised" is a subtle word when I'd found out that she would be speaking to a group of Christian women. I'd have been surprised if I'd been told that she would have been addressing a Sunday school class of more than six. When I heard that she would be speaking to a group of more than two hundred women, it was as if someone had slapped me on the back hard enough to take the breath out of me. I was not surprised, I was shocked.

The day of the event, Jane dressed in a white knit outfit, corrected her makeup and came downstairs. "How do I look?" she asked.

Before the trip to Chapel Hill, Jane had lost down from her normal weight of around 140 pounds to just over 100 pounds At five-foot-seven, she'd looked almost like she'd just been rescued from an Ethiopian refugee camp. During those days in the hospital, however, she had actually gained weight and had gotten back up close to 125 pounds. Fortunately for her, she had been able to maintain the weight gain and that day, she looked fabulous.

"You look wonderful," I said. "Nervous?"

"No. Not really. God is with me and if I stumble, He'll just pick me up and take over." With that, she turned and headed for the door. Before she left, she turned back around and looked at me. "Skip, I love you."

"Me, too," I said as I watched her walk out.

The luncheon was set for noon and I followed her into town shortly after she left. By the time I reached my office, which is located next door to the Sheraton, it was almost 11:45 a.m. and a couple of my co-workers were walking toward the hotel. "We can't wait to hear Jane speak," one of them called over to me as the group continued on their way.

For as much as I wanted to hear Jane's testimony, we'd both agreed that it would be best that I did not attend. At any rate, the audience was to be made up of women, with Pastor Powell, who was to give the invocation, being the only male.

For the next forty-five minutes, I fumbled around my office, constantly looking over at the hotel. I tried to make phone calls, only to embarrass myself by forgetting why I'd made the call. I picked up folders only to lose them in plain sight on my desk. My concentration level had dropped to zero. I was a basket case. Inside, I was dying to hear what Jane would be saying.

Finally, I couldn't stand it anymore. Hesitantly, I walked over next door. When I arrived at the ballroom, the doors to the foyer were shut. At first, I thought that I'd procrastinated too long and was too late. As I peered through the crack between the first two doors, I saw Pastor Powell and Jane sitting at the head table. *Whew,* I thought. *Thank God she hasn't started yet.* Just out of view, I heard someone introduce Jane followed by applause.

I quickly moved to the second pair of doors where I could see the lectern and watched as Jane approached it. She slowly took her position at the podium, bowed her head and asked the rest to join her in a word of prayer. When she finished, she picked up the microphone, moved to the side of the podium and— without notes—addressed the assembly. For the next thirty minutes, Jane took on the grace, appearance and lecturing style of an Anne Graham Lotz; poised and confident. Never once did her grammar or delivery falter.

One moment, the audience was in tears and the next they would break into uncontrolled laughter. Jane had them in the palm of her hand. I have spent the better part of my years as a writer speaking to large groups, usually without a single nervous moment. I've often said, give me a microphone, a room full of people and twenty minutes, and I can talk about anything. But this day as I stood outside the ballroom of The Sheraton Hotel listening to my wife talk from her heart about her experience and her walk with God, I knew I was listening to more. God had taken over and Jane had become his vessel.

Just as Jane began to sum up her remarks, a hotel worker happened upon me as I stood listening through the door. As he approached, he did not even have to ask the question, *What are you doing?* It was written all over his face. Through sobs and tears, all I could say was, "That's my wife in there." The worker shook his head and walked away as I continued to cry for joy.

That one day, I'm sure that Jane touched more hearts than I have done with any column or book that I've ever written. The change that God had made in her was not just evident to me, it was evident to all who now knew her. What she'd experienced those six days in ICU had changed her, a change she wanted all to know about. God had truly entered her heart and she could not get enough of Him. For the rest of her life, her morning prayer would be "God, how can I serve you better this day?"

When Jane finally finished her remarks, the room burst into a thunderous applause and a standing ovation. As I watched her walk back to the head table, I stood in the hallway and wept.

Chapter
14

*J*ANE'S TESTIMONY that December day was never recorded on a machine but it was recorded in a far more important place; on the hearts of those who were there. A little over a year after I started writing this story, I was cleaning out a drawer. In it I found two cassettes. Just as I was about to throw them in the trash, that little voice of mine whispered, "Take a listen." So I set them aside. A couple of weeks later, I found them again, but this time, I decided to take a listen. When I heard Jane's voice, the hair on my arms stood up. I had accidentally stumbled onto the practice tapes she'd used to prepare her speech. Was it really an accident? I think not. I choose to believe that again it was God at work in my life. Not the *mysterious* God but the *determined* God.

The first tape was more of an outline. As she talked to herself, Jane used the tapes to help her decide what to say in an opening and closing prayer, then how to structure the body of her speech. As I played the second tape, I knew what I had was a true gift from God. It was on that tape that Jane had rehearsed her final run. She had punched the record button and had given her speech to an audience made up of our two dogs, Thumper and Little Mutt. As I listened, what I heard was almost verbatim to the speech I'd heard through the doors that day in the hall at the Sheraton.

It is with joy that I can share some of what she had to say that day.

Jane began by telling the audience that there was a time in her life that she would have not been able to stand before a group of any size and tell her story, not just that her shyness or her physical frailness would have gotten in the way, she let it be known that until now, her faith—or better, her lack of faith—would have prevented it.

She started right in by saying that only God can create a miracle and that she herself was living proof of God's miraculous work. She said, "I know beyond a shadow of doubt that I have been touched by the hand of God."

As I listened to Jane tell her story, I began to relive it in vivid details. It's been said that when someone is facing death, their entire life passes before them in an instant. As Jane talked, the times she described swept through me as if a movie was being played on fast-forward right before my eyes. I relived the times she'd almost died, the hospital visits, her pain and her frailty as she continued to lose weight and the fear that consumed us both. At times I had to stop the tape so I could regain my composure. It was like living it all over again. But this time, I got to see it through Jane's eyes.

As she continued her story, she told of her awakening from the coma. It was at that time the fear left her forever. As she awakened in the unfamiliar surroundings and as the cobwebs had been swept from her mind, all fear was swept away as well. She said that she had been wrapped up into the arms of God and given a peace that passed all understanding.

Jane compared the feeling to when she was a child and had a nightmare. Her mom would come into her room and crawl in bed with her. Only then, in the safety of her mother's arms, could she fall back to sleep. At that moment, wrapped up in the loving arms of God, Jane said she knew that she was safe forever.

"There was no fear lying in that bed," she said, "because I knew that God had a plan for me."

I knew that Jane was a Christian. I'd been with her when she'd joined the church and was baptized, but I'd never really heard her speak of an instant or the occasion when she'd given her life to Christ, or as the Baptists call it, "been saved." For me the moment will forever been engrained into my being. I can remember the time, the place, and the very second that I'd felt the hand of God touch my heart and draw me to the altar at Centenary Methodist Church. But for Jane, I'd never heard her speak of it.

If I'd ever had any doubt about Jane's commitment, it disappeared forever as I continued listening to the tape. Jane recalled the night after she'd been taken from ICU to a room in the main hospital. She remembered that shortly after Debby and I had left for the evening that she'd drifted off to sleep. When she awoke in the quiet darkness of her room, she remembered praying, "Oh God, I hope that the peace is still there. Then I heard God's voice say. 'You'll never go back. The peace will be with you forever, and I will be with you forever.'" Pausing for a second, Jane continued, "I held up my hand and said, 'Dear God, I am holding up the white flag of my life and I surrender my all to you. Oh God, you have the keys to my soul and all that I am. And I will walk meekly and humbly where ever you lead me. I take all my misgivings and all my poor choices and I lay them at the foot of the cross. Oh dear God, what a blessing to know that Jesus Christ is in me and that I am forgiven.'" Jane had not only given her life to Christ and I believe to this day that she had touched the hand of God.

As she continued, Jane told of her plan to move forward with her faith and her search to learn more about God. She confessed that although she'd been a member of a church, she had not been a regular participant or a part of that church. Jane said that she felt that she had to find a congregation that would help her to feel comfortable in her baby steps toward finding out all that she could about God. For her, that place became Garber United Methodist Church.

Her next step, Jane said, was to find out all about God that she could. She told the audience that she had an overwhelming desire to study the Bible, so she joined a Bible study group.

"Joining that group was like entering the first grade on the first day of school—both exciting and overpowering all at the same time. But that decision not only allowed me to start my road toward strengthening my faith, it introduced me to a group of women with similar desires and goals," Jane said.

It was those steps that helped to forge her unshakable faith, she added. To be called a Jesus Freak or born-again Christian, a tag she'd shuddered to have been placed on her in a previous life, no longer mattered to her. Jane's quest to run to God and serve Him better, had begun.

"My faith is now unshakable," she said. "All I want to do now is to use my hands and my words to make a difference."

As I continued to listen to the tape, it was as if somehow Jane knew that one day I'd pick the tape up and play it. I felt as if she was speaking directly to me. From the time that she'd come home from Chapel Hill until the day she spoke to the Christian Women, Jane's life had been anything but a bed of roses. Although her health seemed to have been slowly improving, she'd faced bouts with and been hospitalized on other occasions. We'd lost our dear little dog Thumper and in what some may call a mere coincidence, Jane's mom died at Thanksgiving—completing a series of family members who had passed on at that same time years before—her sister and her father.

Yet, Jane's faith remained steadfast. What she revealed to me on that tape and to the others that day in her speech, is best expressed in her own words. "And I pray that each one of you will surrender your life to God. Just walk out of here and say 'Hey God, you can take it; I just can't do it anymore.' And when those mountains come and they will come, because life is not fair and God never said it would be. When those mountains come and the pain and the sadness of losing a loved one, you can look to the heavens and say, 'Lord I need you, I need you all the time but I really need you right now.' I can assure you it's like in the poem *Footprints*, He will pick you up and He will carry you through it. When those around you ask, how did you get through it? You can say, I didn't do anything, God did it." In that moment I knew that Jane knew.

In closing, she offered a final prayer, "May we embrace the child that is within each of us and recognize that this child is indeed a divine spiritual child," she continued. "Our Heavenly Father, we pray for those who are suffering and sick. We pray for those who are in pain. And we pray for all those caretakers, sitting in the hospital rooms all across this country watching their loved ones suffer. We pray that they will be released into your arms and that the angels of comfort and the angels of strength be with them. And Father, we pray as we leave this place today that we will look to the sky and ask Almighty God, 'What can I do for you today?'" That last sentence would be the first words out of Jane's mouth as she began each of the remaining days of her life.

Chapter 15

*T*WO CHRISTMASES and one Thanksgiving would pass and along with each season and each day, Jane's condition continued to improve. With each visit to Chapel Hill, her numbers decreased. She gained weight, her diet and exercise and overall attention to her health began to pay off—so much so that our quarterly visits to Chapel Hill were reduced to semi-annual visits. Because of the portal bi-pass operation she'd had in the years of her diagnosis, Jane would be forever required to take Lactulose in order to ward off bouts with encephalopathy, which still plagued her from time to time. The good news was the bouts were becoming less frequent and I was also better at recognizing the signs that would lead her there and, with just an increase in the frequency of her medicine, could ward them off completely.

Jane immersed herself into her internet business, *The Mailbox Lady,* and into her bible study. Her hand-painted mailboxes that were now in homes all over America seemed to grow in brilliance, not just of color but also in design. In her studio, she filled orders, got to know her customers and busied herself as she listened to what I found later was a huge collection of praise music. Although self-taught, Jane had developed into a masterful artist. Her designs seemed almost alive. I once remarked, as she finished painting a

Golden Retriever on a mailbox that would eventually wind up in the Hamptons, that the dog seemed so real that its eyes followed me around the room. For the first time in over three years, Jane and I had hope. Although we never really looked past the present day, for me, I was actually thinking of the future; a future that I might be able to share with Jane and fulfill the promise we'd made to one another that June day in 1968—a promise to grow old together.

On July 14, 2005, Jane and I made our scheduled trip back to Chapel Hill. After a series of tests, including an MRI and an ultra-sound, we were led into an examining room to meet once again with Dr. Zacks. As the little Napoleon—the name he was called behind his back—entered the room, I saw something I'd never seen in his face before, a remnant of a smile. That afternoon, Dr. Zacks informed us that Jane's numbers had slipped below 10 and were now hovering in the range between 7 and 8.

"You mean—?" I choked on the question.

"That's right, Mr. Crayton," Dr. Zacks interrupted. "Mrs. Crayton's numbers are so low that her chance of survival is far greater than the risk of a transplant." Dr. Zacks placed his file on the table next to Jane and continued. "Mrs. Crayton's liver function has improved so dramatically over the last three years that eventually we believe that she will be taken off the transplant list, which is basically what her numbers indicate today."

As I looked away from the doctor, over to Jane, my eyes welled with tears of joy. Unlike mine, her eyes sparkled and she grinned like a little girl seeing her daddy walk in with a big surprise. "Then what's next?" she asked.

"As long as you're listed, you have the choice of allowing us to release you completely to Dr. Byrd's care or you can continue to come back here for yearly visits. That will be your call."

"Dr. Zacks," I quickly interjected. "No, we want to continue to come back here. Jane sees Dr. Byrd every couple of months, but we still want to see you, should anything go back in the other direction. You've just done wonders bringing my girl back to me. This might sound trite to you, but one of my favorite sayings is 'if it ain't broke, don't fix it.' "

"As you wish," he said. "But as for Mrs. Crayton's improved condition, I've just pointed the way. She's the one who's done all the work."

Before he left, Dr. Zacks told Jane that he wanted to start weaning her off some of the medication and that he wanted her to stop using one of the diuretics, a drug designed to reduce fluids.

As we walked hand-in-hand across the marble floor in the main lobby of the hospital, I flashed back to all the times I had listlessly moped my way past that confounded perpetual-motion machine. I'm sure its presence was there for delight and amusement, but for me, it's pinging and whirring only carried memories of fear and concern. But this day was different. Instead of hearing the pings and plunks, the machine seemed to be chiming and tinkling a happy song. As we left the building, I turned back to the machine I'd become so accustomed to, took a deep breath and slowly let if out. *At least I won't have to listen to you again for a whole year*, I thought. How wrong I was that day.

Chapter
16

HE DRIVE BACK that day was not unlike the drive home we'd made some three years earlier—full of hope and excitement. For the first time in almost four years, the chance that we just might have the opportunity for a future together loomed on the horizon.

Although it had been only a few weeks since Jane and I had spent some time at the beach, we decided that we owed ourselves a little vacation—just the two of us. The first week in August, we loaded up the car, placed Little Mutt in the back seat and headed for Atlantic Beach. Since it would be somewhat of a working vacation for me in that I would have to come into the office a few times over the week, Jane took along two mailboxes she'd promised to paint just to keep her company. Painting mailboxes was anything but work for her; more therapy than anything else. To her, creating a work of art was far more rewarding than curling up with a good book.

That week, we basked in the laziness that time off affords. Most days we'd sleep until 10 or 10:30 then slowly make our way out to the beach. As I sat under an umbrella, Jane would take her chair to the water's edge and let the cool Atlantic slowly wash over her legs.

After lunch we'd rest on the couch or, on occasion, crawl into the bed for an hour. Mid-afternoon ushered in a walk on the beach. Little Mutt and I trailed behind as Jane led the way with her small bucket, stopping from time to time to fill it with smooth rocks for her fish pond back home. Next to the beach, that pond in our backyard was Jane's favorite place in the world. It was a place where she sat and studied her bible, and I'm sure, lost herself deep in thought.

We seldom went out for dinner. Most evenings, I'd cook while Jane hummed and worked away on a mailbox. And after dinner, we'd sit outside and rock, Little Mutt snuggled in one of our laps, and watch as the stars turned evening into night. The mundane of those days seemed so rewarding after the roller coaster ride we'd been on for the past few years. I don't think I'd ever welcomed boredom with such enthusiasm.

On Wednesday, I had to leave early for an office meeting, but I assured Jane that I'd be back before lunch. When I called her around 11:00 a.m. and told her that something I had to attend to would keep me until 2:30 or 3:00 p.m., Jane told me that she was fine and to take my time. All I wanted to do was to get back to her.

It was almost 3:30 p.m. before I parked my car under the beach house. I reached into the back seat and fetched some fresh vegetables I'd picked up at a produce market in Newport on the way through. When I opened the door to the beach house, I heard Little Mutt barking from the bedroom. Quietly I set my groceries down, slipped out of my pants and cracked the bedroom door. Little Mutt quickly sat up, her tail keeping time with the ceiling fan. Jane appeared to be sleeping so I quietly slipped into the bed and snuggled up next to her. That's when I noticed that she'd been crying.

"What's wrong?" I whispered.

"Nothing!" she answered.

"Jane." I raised slightly and said, "You know we stopped playing that game a long time ago. You don't just cry for no reason. Tell me what's wrong."

Without turning she sniffled, "I had a premonition."

"About what?" I asked.

"That I'm going to die."

My heart dissolved and puddled around my feet. It was as if I'd had the same déjà vu. I wrapped my arms around her and held her tightly. For a couple of minutes neither of us said a word. My mind raced trying to figure out what to say next—how to fix everything.

"Baby," I finally said. "It was only a dream. You're not going to die. Dr. Zacks has just given you your wings. He almost smiled when he told us. Think about it, baby, we can finally look to tomorrow."

Slowly, I watched her unfold and turn toward me. "I guess you're right, but it all seems so real."

"You mean *seemed* so real," I suggested.

"Okay, seemed," she said. "Maybe you're right. I guess it could be just that I've lived under a death sentence for so long that, now that I've been given a reprieve, I don't want to go back. I want it to be real."

"Don't be afraid." I looked into her eyes and stroked her hair. "Everything is going to be just fine."

"Oh, I'm not afraid, especially of dying. I know where I'll be going when the time comes. It's just that, Skip, I don't want to leave you. I know how much you truly love me and I dare to think of the pain you'll go through when it happens. I don't know what you will do."

Chapter 17

HE NEXT DAY we got up and headed down east to Jimmy and Patti's place on Adam's Creek. When we arrived, Jimmy handed me a beer and directed us to his boat, idling at the end of his dock. Patti was already on board. As we walked along the dock, Jimmy—in his always upbeat manner—said, "It's such a beautiful day, Patti and I decided it would be great to take the boat across the river to Oriental and have lunch."

I looked at Jane and we both smiled. It had been years since we'd both been out on the Neuse River together at the same time. "Sounds like a plan," I said as I winked at Jane.

Once on board, we left the dock and headed down Adam's Creek and out onto the Neuse River. Just five miles away on the other side sat the village of Oriental, North Carolina. Once a quiet fishing village whose fleet of shrimp boats outnumbered the homes that clustered close to the waterfront, fishing had given way to sailing. Because of its location on the widest river in America with an average daily wind count second only to San Francisco Bay; this sleepy little town had evolved into "The Sailing Capital of North Carolina." Now sailboats not only outnumbered the number of homes in Oriental, they outnumbered the residents as well. And gone forever was the Down East "high-tider" brogue spoken by most natives, replaced by accents from New Jersey and Raleigh.

As we crossed the river, Jane sat back and seemed to slip away into a trance-like connection with all her senses. Deep breaths followed by glances up and down the river convinced me that she was taking it all in; the cobalt blue of the river, touched in the distance by the pale blue sky, the sea birds squealing overhead and the fresh smell of salt that could only be found in the river in late summer. It was as if the day was being captured and tucked away into some very private place within her soul.

As we slowed to enter the harbor, Jane stood up and made her way next to me. Placing her arm around my waist and kissing me on the neck, she asked," Do you remember the first time we came into this harbor?"

It seemed like centuries—no—a lifetime since we'd taken our little twenty-seven-foot sailboat and made the trip from New Bern to Oriental, entering the harbor just as the sun was going down. Oh how so much had changed and how young and naïve we'd both been.

"Still looks pretty much the same," I said. "Except for all the boats."

"I'm glad we did that. The sailing I mean," she said. "I'm glad we shared those times."

"Me too," I said. "Now that you're better, maybe we can do it again."

"This time let's do it on a power boat," she said as she popped me on the butt. "You're getting too old for a sailboat."

After we tied up at the town dock, the four of us made our way around the corner to one of the many waterfront restaurants for lunch. In the "old days" there were only two places open for lunch, but Oriental had grown up in many respects and now was catering to yuppies and retirees instead of the fried seafood crowd. With the new customers came bistros with hanging ferns and tofu. The place we picked was somewhere in the middle. Along with a crab cake sandwich, they also offered burgers.

When lunch was over, we divided into twos—Jimmy and I went one way and Jane and Patti the other. I can still see them skipping down Hodges Street like two little girls as they headed for a dress shop that had just opened.

An hour later, Jimmy and Patti's boat, *The Peppermint,* idled slowly out of the harbor. Jane opened her bag and showed me the two new dresses she'd bought. As she placed each one in front her, she whirled around and giggled. Her smile dazzled me and her excitement rubbed off on all of us. As we headed back across the river, the premonition of the previous day had slipped away, replaced by the hope that now a new day had begun. For the first time, we might even be able to travel some. Maybe to England, a dream we'd both shared, or even back to Jamaica, a place we both loved and missed. God had granted us a new beginning. A new day had indeed dawned and our life together was starting all over again.

Chapter 18

*W*E LEFT THE BEACH early on Friday. Saturday night was our supper club and new member Nancy Stallings would be hosting it at her condo overlooking the Trent River. On the way home, as Little Mutt dozed in her lap, Jane complained of feeling just a bit uncomfortable. When I asked her to describe the feeling, she told me that it was as if she hadn't slept at all the night before; she felt tired and uneasy.

"Do you think it has anything to do with your liver?" I asked.

"No," she said. "I've never felt quite like this before."

When we arrived home, Jane walked over to the couch to lie down. Her frailty and illness left most of the loading and unloading up to me, but she did try to do as much to help as possible. But for her to go directly to the couch and lie down was so unlike her. Leaving Little Mutt in the back yard, I followed her to the family room. "What's wrong?" I asked.

"I don't know," she responded. "It's just that I'm so tired. You go on and finish unloading the car. I must have overdone it a little yesterday. If I lie here a while, maybe it will go away."

When I finished putting the bags away and retrieved Little Mutt from the backyard, I went again to check on Jane. By the time I reached the couch I found her sleeping restlessly. But she was asleep so I sat down on the facing couch and turned on the TV. Moments later we were all three snoring.

When I awoke an hour and a half later, I looked across at Jane, staring at me from the other couch. For a moment that Sunday in June, three years earlier flashed across my mind and I quickly leaned forward.

Jane smiled. "I didn't mean to scare you."

"How long you been awake?" I asked, brushing the crumbs from my eyes.

"Oh, I didn't sleep very long. It's like I'm so tired but I can't seem to catch my breath."

I sat up and rolled my neck, popping sounds clicked through my shoulders. "You want me to call the doctor?"

"It's after five and they'll only want me to go to the emergency room and you know what Fridays can be like there. We'll just sit over in the corner for five hours while they take care of all the stabbings and gunshots. Anyway, I want to see Ron or one of his partners, not some contract ER doc."

"Are you sure?" I got up and went to the bar to pour a glass of wine.

"This is probably nothing," she said. "Anyway, I'll probably be okay in the morning and if not we'll call Ron."

I placed the wine bottle back in the ice machine, picked my wineglass, walked over to Jane and kissed her on the forehead. "You feel like eating something?" Jane nodded. "Okay, you lay right there and try and get some rest. I'll walk Little Mutt and get supper started." As I walked toward the door the nagging feeling that had so quickly disappeared the day before in Oriental began to steal its way back into my mind. *She's going to be all right,* I told myself. Dr. Zacks told us so himself. There's got to be some simple answer to all of this.

After dinner, we watched some TV then turned in early. Jane seemed, at least to me, to be a little better. The next morning we slept until 11:00 a.m. When Jane finally shook me awake she told me to call Ron, she said she was actually feeling worse—the shortness in her breath had not gotten any better.

On the way to the hospital, her premonition jumped to center stage again. "Skip, when I die I want to be buried in that little silver cross you gave me for Christmas last year."

"What!" I exclaimed. "Baby, we've been over this before. Dr. Zacks told us both, you're going to be all right."

"It's in my jewelry box, on the first shelf," she continued as if she'd not heard a word.

"Damn it, Jane." I flashed my eyes toward her. "Let's don't go there. You're going to be just fine. One of Ron's partners is waiting for us at the emergency room, he'll figure all this out and we'll be on our way back home in no time."

Jane had been right about one thing, the ER at noon is not nearly as active as at midnight, especially on a Saturday. Moments after we arrived, the triage nurse examined her and she was quickly taken back into a room. As expected, the doctor showed up shortly and examined her. What he found was that Jane had some fluid in her lungs. When he asked if there had been any recent changes in her medication, a lightning bolt went off and jolted my senses. *The diuretic.* Now it all made sense to me.

As I told the ER doctor about our recent visit to Chapel Hill and the results of that visit, it seemed to make sense to him as well. The absence of the diuretic from Jane's critically balanced group of meds had caused her to retain fluid, and that fluid had gathered around her heart. Surely, a diuretic shot and the return to her previous dosage would bring her back to normal

86

in a couple of days. I was told to expect her to pee a lot over the next few days.

What a relief I felt as I turned into our driveway. "Feel better?" I asked as I opened her car door.

"I guess so," she said. "At least we know what caused it."

"I knew it had to be something simple. The minute he mentioned fluid, I knew the answer." We'd been walking on eggshells for so many years that, with her release a few weeks earlier by Dr. Zacks, we still were apprehensive, as though waiting for the other shoe to drop. Finally, I allowed myself to let out a breath. I now believed that I could see light at the end of the tunnel.

Chapter
19

*J*ANE DECIDED NOT TO ATTEND the supper club gathering that night. Although she'd been to the bathroom while still in the ER, she had not gone much since we'd returned home. When I called Nancy and told her that we would not be able to come, Jane quickly interrupted me and told me to tell Nancy that I would be attending. When I told Jane that I felt that I needed to be with her, my protests fell on deaf ears.

"What are you going to be able to do?" she asked. "Go on and have a good time."

Reluctantly, I went to Nancy's, but my heart was at home. My concern for Jane made me a poor dinner partner. I didn't think that Jane was passing enough water to reduce the fluid in her lungs. Between cocktails and dinner, I slipped outside and called Ron. When I got his machine, I left a message and my worrying continued.

After dinner, I didn't wait for desert. I bid my goodbyes and started home. About halfway to the house, my cell phone rang. Ron told me to increase the dosage and to bring Jane in on Monday if nothing had changed. Ron again told me not to worry, that the increase should do the trick. *That damn premonition, why was it chopping away at me? Why couldn't I get it out of my mind?*

Sunday passed into Sunday night and it appeared to me that Jane was getting worse. Not much of a complainer, she continued to tell me how uncomfortable she was. That she didn't feel rested and just felt bad all over.

On Sunday night, the strangest thing happened. As Jane rested on the couch, the phone rang. It was Dr. Zacks. In the more than three years that I had known him, I had never talked to Steven Zacks anywhere other than at Chapel Hill. He had never called before. He apologized for the late hour, it was almost ten o'clock, and told me that he was still at the hospital and was reviewing Jane's chart. I've been told that I have a very sharp memory, but if today someone offered me a million dollars to remember the reason Dr. Zacks had called, I couldn't do it. All I can recall is that before Dr. Zacks hung up, I told him about Jane's condition and that Dr. Wilkins felt that the cause of the fluid must have come from the deletion of the diuretic drug. What happened next floored me. Dr. Zacks began to apologize profusely. It was so out of character, or maybe out of what I perceived his character to be. Hearing him apologize seemed as out of place as an Arab at a bar mitzvah. That caring trace of a smile that we'd noticed was for real. This man, who came across so disconnected and aloof from his patients, really cared.

When I hung up, again I was convinced that once Jane's drugs had been regulated, everything would be okay. That would all change on Monday morning as my second nightmare began.

PART TWO

"God, you promised me, that if I followed you, you would be with me always. But I have noticed that during the most trying periods of my life, there have only been one set of footprints in the sand. Why, when I needed you most, have you not been there for me?"

"My son, my precious child, I love you and I would never leave you. During your times of trial and suffering, when you have seen only one set of footprints, it was then that I carried you."
"Oh thank you God," I said. "Why now as you carry me through the most troubled time of my life, do I look down and see more and more footprints walking with you?"

"Child, those are the footprints of your friends, who have come to help me carry you through your time of need."

—Paraphrased from Footprints in the Sand by Mary Stevenson

Chapter
20

IRST THING MONDAY MORNING, I called Ron and told him what was going on. He immediately told me to get Jane over to his office. Ron's nurse LaRue, a petite blonde with haunting blue eyes, has been with him as long as I can remember. She is as efficient an RN as there can be, but what takes her to the next level is her compassion for her patients. We had not been seated in the waiting room two minutes when LaRue called us back. I followed Jane to the nurses' station and sat quietly as she checked Jane's vitals. As I sat staring around the room, I missed the concerned look on her face as LaRue checked Jane's pulse again then abruptly dashed off down the hall towards Ron's office. LaRue had barely disappeared through the door when Ron burst into the hall with his nurse in tow.

"Get an ambulance!" he shouted over his shoulder, "and tell them to hurry."

I could feel the blood rush from my face as I dashed to Jane's side. "Ron, what's wrong?"

"Here, Skip, help me get her into an examining room, we need to get her off her feet." Ron's doctor-face was all over him. This old drinking buddy of mine was all business.

"What's wrong?" I insisted.

"Her resting pulse rate is 130," he said. "You have any clue how long she's been like this?"

"I told you Saturday night when we talked that she didn't feel good. That's why we came in this morning." I said. "What's wrong?"

"We've got to get her to the hospital and get that rate down. That's all I know right now. Go sit in my office and I'll call you when she's ready to be transported."

As I sat in Ron's office, it all started coming back to me again: alone in a hospital setting, Ron with Jane, things not looking good. *Had the last three years just been a dream? Would I have to face this nightmare all over again? Would there be a light at the end of the tunnel or would it be a train barreling down upon me at full speed?* Those thoughts and many more flooded my mind.

For what seemed like hours, I sat in Ron's office and thought. Finally, Ron walked in and told me that Jane was outside in an ambulance. He showed me to the back door and told me the ambulance was just outside.

"What is it?" I asked.

A confused look came across Ron's face. "It looks like it's her heart."

"Her heart." I froze. "They made sure that there was nothing wrong with her heart back at Chapel Hill. They stressed it out and everything. She would have never made the transplant list if there had even been a hint of a problem with her heart." I shook my head, "I just don't understand."

"This looks like something new," Ron said as he walked me over to the ambulance. "We have a new cardiologist who works full time at the hospital. He's waiting for them to bring Jane over. He'll get to the bottom of this. Get in and tell her that you love her and then follow them to the hospital."

Ron opened the side door to the ambulance, patted me on the shoulder, then walked back to his office.

When I stepped into the ambulance, two attendants were hooking up IV's and talking with the hospital by way of a two-way radio. "Am I in the way?"

"No, not at all. Sit right here," the EMT tech said and pointed to a little seat next to Jane.

"Hey, princess." I placed my hand on her shoulder and leaned over and kissed her on the cheek.

Jane smiled back at me. There was a peace about her I cannot express in words, only that she seemed to be bathed in a warm glow that radiated all around her. "It's going to be okay. They say it's my heart. It's beating too fast. This nice man is getting ready to give me a drug that will bring my heart rate down then we'll go to the hospital. I want you to ride over there with me, okay?"

"Sure, sweetie, whatever you want." I stroked her hair.

"I'm sorry," the EMT tech interrupted. "It'll be best if you follow us over."

"But she wants me with her," I protested.

Jane reached up and touched my hand. "It'll be alright, baby. If that's what the nice man wants, do what he says. Anyway, we're only five minutes away."

I raised my trembling hand and brushed my hair back. "Okay, but I want to sit here with you until they are ready to leave." The tech nodded his approval.

On the way to the hospital, I called my angel, my sister Debby, to tell her that Jane was on the way to the hospital. Before I could tell her what had happened, Debby interrupted me. "I thought they'd just about cut her loose," she said.

"It's not her liver," I said. "It's her heart."

"What?" I had to hold the phone away from my ear. I believe the person in the car behind me could have heard Debby's question.

"It's her heart. Ron says it's beating like 130 beats a minute and they can't get it down."

95

"Didn't she used to have tachycardia?" Debby asked.

"Yeah, I'd forgotten about that. Her heart would start racing but if she pushed on her eyes, it would eventually stop. In fact, Ron's old partner, who was Jane's doctor before he retired, used to want to see her when she had an attack, but I could never get her over to his office before the episode would be over and her heart rate would be back to normal." For a moment, a sense of relief washed over me. "Maybe that's all this is."

"Where are you?" Debby asked.

"I'm behind the ambulance."

"I'll see you in a short," Debby said in a hurry and hung up.

When I finished talking with my sister, I called Patti and Annie Parker to let them know what was happening. I asked them both to go by and see Jane as soon as they could. I knew Patti would have to come in from her summer place, but Annie could get over right away.

Chapter
21

S SOON AS JANE GOT SITUATED in the Cardiac Care Unit, Annie showed up. Dr. Win, the attending cardiologist continued to work on reducing Jane's heart rate. And all the while, Jane, lying in bed with an angelic look on her face, seemed to be aware of everything and in total control. It was as if she had not just played out the scene before, she was aware of the outcome.

I was relieved when Annie arrived. There were some things that I needed to attend to, but I did not want to leave Jane. Both Annie and Jane encouraged me to go look after what needed to be taken care of and I was assured that Annie would be there. Anyway, as Jane had said, there were tests to be made and we probably wouldn't know anything until the doctors made their rounds.

I quickly went home and walked Little Mutt. Then I went to the office to let them know what was happening and to not expect me for a day or two. On the way out the door, one of my clients met me and asked if we could talk for just a moment. For some strange reason, I agreed. As I led him to the conference room, a series of déjà vu played out before me like an old movie. It felt as though every word he said, every gesture or move he made, I had witnessed before. It was as if I could predict his every move and word, before it took place.

The entire event lasted until he walked out the door. I can't say whether it scared me or not, but it moved me so much that I had to sit down and catch my breath. My little voice no longer whispered to me, it screamed for me to get back to the hospital.

When I walked into Jane's room, Dr. Win was sitting on her bed. My sister sat in the corner and looked up at me then back down at the floor. Debby's reaction, the look on Dr. Win's face and the red in Annie's eyes told me that the news was going to be bad.

"What's wrong?" I stumbled over to Jane and took her hand in mine.

"It's my heart," she said. "Let this good-looking doc tell you about it."

"I wish I was a little older," the doctor kidded. "I'd give Mr. Crayton a run for his money."

"You might be cute, Dr. Win, but there's no way I'd let you catch me. He's been my guy way too long for me to ever let him go."

Dr. Win smiled and patted Jane on the leg. "I'm going to take Mr. Crayton out in the hall and fill him in. We'll be back in a minute or two."

Jane sat up. "You're not keeping anything from me, are you?"

"No, Mrs. Crayton," the doctor assured Jane. "There's a blackboard at the nurses' station and it will be easier for me to draw out what's going on. I guarantee there's nothing more to tell."

I followed Dr. Win to the nurses' station and sat down on one of the rolling stools. As he drew a circle, he showed me where the heart valves were located. Apparently Jane's heart was not opening and closing fully, only about twenty-five percent. This, along with an extended period of accelerated heart beats had caused a tear in one of the two valves and now it would not fully close. Dr. Win told me that Jane had somehow contracted a heart virus, probably while we'd been at the beach and that the virus had damaged her heart.

When he'd finished, he told me that he'd explained it all to Jane and that she fully understood her condition. Then he asked if I had any questions.

During the past three years, I'd wished that Jane's illness had been with her heart instead of her liver. There were so many ways that a damaged heart could be repaired. But the only remedy that had been given to her condition was either a miracle that her liver would rebound, at least partially, or a transplant. On July 17, just three short weeks before, we'd been given that miracle.

Heart surgery, at least as I understood it, was almost as routine as setting a broken arm. Heck, they even did open heart surgery right there at Craven Regional.

"You're going to fix it, aren't you?" I said as if it were as simple as changing a tire.

When Dr. Win answered me, my heart fell and splattered on the floor. "It's not that easy, Mr. Crayton. I'm not sure we can."

"But, but, but it's done all the time," I stuttered. "There's a guy right here at Craven who does it every day."

Dr. Win reached over and patted me on my arm. "Your wife's heart has enlarged. To put it in layman's terms, the flap that closes on the valve is too small for the hole. That, along with the fact that Mrs. Crayton's heart is beating at only twenty-five percent efficiency means that, in my opinion, she would never survive the operation. Even if they could repair the valve, when they tried to take her off the machine, her heart probably would not restart."

Our roller coaster of a life had started back down the hill. The blood ran from my face and my hands trembled. What air I had in my lungs slipped out in a quiet sigh.

"There's got to be something we can do." I brushed my hair back and shook my head. Tears once again filled my eyes.

"Dr. Moore and I will be talking about our options when he comes by during rounds. But Mr. Crayton, I want you to understand that whatever we can do for Mrs. Crayton, her lifestyle and her quality of life are going be greatly affected. She may be bound to a wheelchair for what is left of her life."

The blood shot back up into my face as I leaned forward. "Doc, you've got to understand, she's all I've got. You just give her back to me. I don't give a damn if she's in a wheelchair. You just give her back to me. I'll take care of her."

Chapter 22

*W*HEN I RETURNED to Jane's room, Annie was still with her. For the first time in almost four years, I didn't know what to do. I didn't have a plan. During Jane's fight with liver disease, there had always been something I could do or say, whether it was pestering the doctors to get her listed or keeping her sodium levels low or helping her with her medicine. There always seemed to be a way for me to show Jane that there was a reason for hope. I guess the washed-out look on my face gave me away when I sat next to her on the bed.

"It's going to be okay," she said.

I squeezed her hand. I garnered a slight smile as I looked into her eyes—eyes that had been green when we'd first married, but now were a smoky blue. "I know, princess," I said. "Just another hurdle in the road. We'll get through this just like we've gotten through all the rest. Trust me."

"Oh, I do trust you, Skip. But this time, I have a feeling that things are going to be different. I think that God has other plans for us." She squeezed my hand.

"Don't be ridiculous," I demanded. "You're going to be just fine."

"Oh my sweet wonderful Skip," she sighed. "You've fought so hard for me. You never give up. You truly are my strength."

"And baby, I'm not through fighting. We're not going to give up. We have more to do, the two of us." I leaned closer. "Don't you give up on me."

"Skip, I'm not going to give up," she said softly. "But we have to face the facts that this is not good."

"You're not going to die," tears streamed down my cheeks. "I just won't let that happen if we have to go to the Mayo Clinic, damn it. You're going to get better."

"Honey, don't you see. I'm not afraid of dying." She stroked my arm and looked deeply into my eyes, as if she could actually see into my soul. "I'm just worried about what will happen to you after I'm gone."

For a moment her words hung in the air, then slowly seeped into my mind, like water into a sponge. "Baby, let's not go there. When Ron gets here, we'll work on our game plan. I'm getting you fixed then we're going to go back home. Trust me."

"Okay, sweetie," Jane surrendered. "Let's find out what Ron has to say."

It was early evening when Ron stuck his head in the room. Dr. Byrd had come by, not as one of her doctors, but as a friend. As sick as Jane was, she flirted with him and as always made him blush. I knew how much Dr. Byrd thought of Jane, and his presence warmed my soul.

After Dr. Byrd bid us his goodbyes, Ron got straight to the point. He mirrored what Dr. Win had said, but modified it by suggesting that we go to another hospital where we could get the most-up-to-date care. He told us that he leaned toward the Brody School of Medicine at East Carolina University in nearby Greenville, a town just forty-five miles from New Bern. Not only did the hospital and medical school boast a heart surgeon Ron called the best heart surgeon on planet earth, but they also had a cardiologist by the name of Dr. Frazier. Frazier had developed a procedure using what was considered at the time, a breakthrough device called a syncopated dual chamber pacemaker. The device could be used to control Jane's heart rate and beat and give her far more mobility than Dr. Win had predicted. Ron told me that he'd talked with Dr. Frazier and that he would accept Jane as a patient. If we agreed, Ron planned to move Jane to Greenville in the morning. Ron was recommending ECU, but it was up to us to make the final decision.

"It's a no-brainer," I said as I smiled at Jane. "You see, I told you Ron would get you fixed right up."

IT WAS ALMOST 11:00 p.m. when I turned into my driveway. Debby had agreed to stay the night with Jane so that I could get some rest. I planned to relieve her the next morning so that she could take care of some personal matters before we'd follow Jane to the hospital at ECU.

As I opened the door, Little Mutt charged through the kitchen and engulfed me as she always did. That night, her loving seemed more special as she licked me all over. Dogs have a way of sensing things. I don't know whether they pick up on our moods or that they can just read our minds, but that night my special little dog became my caretaker as I held onto her tightly and sobbed. As much as I'd tried to find a bright spot in Ron's words, I'd known him too long and too well. My gut told me that the move to Greenville would be a long shot at best.

The last thing Jane asked me to do before I left the hospital was to call Peggy when I got home. Peggy Flowers was one of Jane's best friends, although their families had lived on opposite sides of the law in Johnston County where Jane's uncle was a famous Superior Court Judge and Peggy's, a famous bootlegger. The two girls had met in college and had quickly put those differences behind them. Their friendship was

103

vast and strong—the kind where physical distances never came between the bond. Through all the years, they'd stayed in touch and each time they got together, they always picked up right where they'd left off.

But calling Peggy was something I'd not looked forward to. Only three months earlier, Peggy's only child, her daughter Alley, and love of her life had been killed in a tragic automobile accident. When Jane heard the news of Alley's death, she dropped everything and went to Peggy, staying with her, even sleeping in the same bed with her throughout the whole funeral ordeal. I'm told that Jane was the only one who could minister comfort to Peggy during that dreadful time.

Peggy's grieving period had just begun, and I feared that telling her that Jane was seriously ill might push her over the edge. Carefully, I called and broke the news. Although I tried to stop her, Peggy said that she would be at the hospital first thing in the morning. She wanted to be with Debby and me when we followed Jane to Greenville.

Chapter 23

*B*Y THE TIME I got to the hospital that Tuesday morning, I had a sense that things were not going to be good. I found Debby wrapped in a blanket, sitting in the waiting room.

"I'm afraid she's not going to recognize you," Debby said, a sullen look on her face.

"What?" I sat down next to her and wiped my face.

"Last night, she began to fret, so they gave her Ambien to quiet her down. It sent her straight into one of her episodes." Debby shook her head.

"Didn't those idiots know that she couldn't take anything like that," I said, hoping I'd wake up the entire hospital. "Why didn't they call me first?"

"They never said a word to me either and I was sleeping right next to her. It was only after she lapsed into la-la land that I realized what was happening, and then it was too late."

"They *are* trying to bring her back to normal, aren't they?" Frustration overcame my anger.

"Yeah, but her high heart rate may slow down her comeback." Debby stood up and eased toward the elevator. "God, I need a cigarette."

"Do you know when they're going to take her to Greenville?" I asked.

"Not soon enough." The elevator door opened and my sister stepped in. "If I didn't know better, I'd say it looks like they're trying to kill her around here."

Just as the door shut, the second elevator door opened and Peggy stepped out. Immediately her eyes found me. "How is she?"

"I haven't been back," I said as she walked over and hugged me. "But Debby said that she had a bad night."

Peggy stepped back and brushed her long blond hair from her face. "Where is she?"

"She's right in there." I pointed to the room. "Do you remember the episode Jane had last year when you spent the weekend with us."

"Remember? Are you kidding? That scared the shit out of me. En-cep-a something, I think you called it."

"Encephalopathy."

Her face contoured in confusion. "Oh my God, not again!"

"Debby said that she fell into it last night. I'm not even sure she'll recognize me."

As Peggy and I slowly entered Jane's room, instead of the child-like symptoms that generally occurred with encephalopathy, this time Jane had slipped deeper into a trance-like condition, just barely on the outskirts of a coma. She knew we were in the room and who we were, but everything else was as if she was wandering around in a dense fog.

An hour later, Ron came by to let us know that the EMT crew was on its way up to get Jane and take her to Greenville. Within minutes they had transferred her and all her IV's to the gurney.

"Do you want to follow us?" one of the techs asked me.

I raised my trembling hands and held them in front of me as if I were pushing against the very air that separated us.

106

"Don't wait on us. I've got to find my sister. You just get her to Greenville as quick as you can, we'll be close behind."

With that, the tech nodded and wheeled my precious Jane out the CCU door. I stood and again watched someone I didn't know carry the person I loved the most in the entire world on another trip she'd never remember. I closed my eyes and prayed that God would give me another miracle.

Peggy and I found Debby and moments later we turned out of the hospital parking lot and began the short ride to Greenville. The road to Greenville was one that I knew well. I had traveled that road hundreds, maybe thousands of times, from the time when Jane was in college, to the years since 1978 when I'd adopted the ECU Pirate football team. To me, it is still the longest forty-three miles in North Carolina. There is no way to get there from New Bern in less than an hour. This day would be no different. The good news was that Pitt was a lot closer than UNC. At least I could thank Chancellor Emeritus Leo Jenkins for that. Without his persistence, there would have never been a medical school at ECU.

It was after nine that night before Dr. Frazier peeped into Jane's room. A small unassuming man with a bright smile, he was considered one of the best cardiologists in the country, especially when it came to working with the new type of pacemaker that Ron had assured me was a real breakthrough in controlling irregular heart rates. The device, Ron had said, was almost custom designed for Jane's condition. It was a miracle in itself that it was available so close to home, with a doctor so well-trained in its application and use.

After a few minutes with Dr. Frazier, I was completely convinced that Ron had pointed us in the right direction. This man, who looked more like a college professor than a doctor, had such an upbeat

107

and positive demeanor that I'd have probably joined an Amway team had he been selling the products. And beside his personality, I admired his work ethic. When most doctors would have been home watching TV or playing with the kids, this man was making rounds, taking time to get to know both patient and family. He made sure that each question that I had was completely answered before we went on to the next one and all but assured me that he'd have Jane out of there in a few days and back to living as close to normal a life as could be expected.

Before he left, Dr. Frazier told us to go home and get some rest. I guess our weary appearance was not hard to ignore. He convinced me that Jane would more than likely sleep through the night and that he'd rather have us alert and well-rested for the next day. How prophetic that advice would become.

Unfortunately, Jane was still drifting around in her semi-coma-like condition, coming in and out of reality. She barely responded when I kissed her and told her that I'd see her in the morning. But meeting Dr. Frazier had re-lit the ember of hope that I'd continued to hold onto for the last four years. As we walked across the parking lot to Debby's car, a sense of well-being swept over me. And once again, the prospect of growing old with Jane at my side appeared on the horizon as the roller coaster bottomed out and began another upward climb. Yet, even with that feeling, I did not sleep well that night.

Chapter
24

*T*HE DRIVE BACK to Greenville the next morning was filled with small talk. I sat in the back seat of my sister's car so the two women could smoke. As we approached Vanceboro, a hamlet that signaled the halfway point, Peggy got noticeably quieter. I could see her eyes and her expressions in the rearview mirror. It was as if a spell had been cast over her. It was as if her hair had turned white.

I placed my hand on her shoulder. Her neck shivered at my touch. "What's wrong?" I asked.

Peggy turned in her seat and looked directly into my eyes. "You know that field we just passed?"

"No, I guess I wasn't paying much attention to anything around us," I said. "Why?"

"In the middle of it, all alone was a black crow."

"Okay, there was a black crow in the middle of a field," I said. "What's that got to do with anything?" I asked as I patted her on the shoulder.

Peggy shuddered. It was as if her body temperature had dropped twenty degrees. Her skin felt like ice. "It's an omen, Skip. A bad omen."

"Come on, Peggy," I tried to reassure her. "You heard the doc just like I did. We're going to get our girl back."

"Gosh, I hope you're right, Skip." Peggy turned back around and lit a cigarette. She said very little the rest of the way to Greenville.

WHEN GOD first whispered the word "pastor" into our vocabulary, he must have had Powell Osteen in mind. More than six feet tall with graying hair and a boyishly kind face, it could have been just as easy to confuse Powell with one of the doctors making rounds at the hospital. Powell loves God. Next in line after his family is his flock. And like the Biblical Sheppard, he knows each one in a personal way. Powell had been with Jane in the days before at Craven Regional so it was no surprise when I came into her room at Pitt and found him sitting next to her bed. Fortunately, Jane had slipped out of her unconsciousness long enough to feel his presence and know that it was Powell who sat beside her.

"Oh Powell. Oh Powell," she cried out, convincing us all that she knew the man had a direct line to God.

Powell smiled as we entered the room. "Have you talked to the doctor?" he asked. "Let's step outside," he said as he turned to Jane. "Jane, I'm going out in the hall for just a moment. I'll be right back. Skip's here with Debby and..."

"Peggy," Debby said.

"And Peggy. We'll be right back in just a moment."

Jane opened her eyes and for a moment smiled at me. "Hey Princess, I'll be right back, okay?"

When we got out into the hall, Powell bit his bottom lip. "I'm afraid things have changed since last night."

Once again, I felt the roller coaster crest the hill and pause at the top. "What do you mean change?"

"I haven't talked to the doctor, only the nurse. She told me that they did an ultrasound of Jane's heart this morning and things have changed. They don't believe that they can put in the pacemaker." A thousand

110

questions stood in line to spew from my mouth, but before I could get even one of them out, Powell interrupted. "Skip, that's all I know. I think you need to talk to the doctor."

Time in a hospital doesn't just creep by, it doesn't just crawl, it moves slower than a turtle crossing a highway. Each tick of the clock seems more like an hour than a second, especially when you're waiting to talk to a doctor. It was after lunch before Dr. Frazier could break free. When he did, he took me into a small room dominated by a computer screen. After a few clicks of the mouse, he brought up a moving image of Jane's heart.

"See those dots in the heart chamber?" He pointed to a random series of dots that seemed to be floating about in the picture. "Those are blood clots in your wife's heart."

"Does that mean that you can't put in the pacemaker?" I asked.

"Mr. Crayton," Dr. Frasier turned from the computer screen, his eyes full of compassion. "I hate to have to tell you this, but at any time, one or all of them could break free, cause a stroke and end your wife's life. Even something as slight as lifting her up in the bed."

The roller coaster crested the hill and shot downward. Only this time there didn't seem to be a bottom at the end of the hill. I place my hand over my mouth trying to stifle the cry I could not withhold. Dr. Frazier sat with me, his hand on my shoulder as I fought to gain control.

As soon as I could form an understandable word, I asked, "Is this it? Is there anything more than just waiting for her to die?" The word "die" trailed off into a whisper.

"There is one long shot," he said. "But because of the condition of her liver and the shape she is in, it is a real long shot. If they're willing to take your wife as a heart transplant patient at UNC, she might have a chance."

Oh, to see that perpetual motion machine again, I thought. *I'll never ever say another bad thing about it. Just to hear those balls whirring and pinging once again would be the prettiest sound in the world.*

"Let's do it," I said.

"I thought you might feel that way, so I've called them and they've agreed to look at her chart. The nurse is emailing the charts to them as we speak." Dr. Frazier got up and walked to the door, stopped, then turned back to me. "Mr. Crayton, I don't want to get your hopes up, but I've never heard of a double heart and liver transplant ever taking place anywhere. This is as long a shot as it gets. It's now in the hands of Dr. Marshall Runge in Chapel Hill."

Chapter
25

*H*OW I FOUND MY WAY BACK to Jane's room through the protective haze that my mind had created is still a mystery. Jane's consciousness meandered in and out with cries of "Oh, Powell," and "I want my mama," the last of which cut so deeply that I could hardly control my tears. After explaining to the others what had taken place with Dr. Frasier, I decided to call Ron. Jane's nurse, I found out, had worked for Ron some years before and confirmed what I already knew, that behind his all-business exterior was the most compassionate of human beings.

Ron Moore and I are close friends. In fact, I may be his closest friend. Yet, I'd never seen him display much emotional sadness. Even the night he and I talked on the phone for hours after the death of his ex-wife and mother of his two girls, I could never really tell whether or not he'd allowed himself to grieve. My phone call that day told a different story. Before I finished telling Ron what Dr. Frazier had said, the phone went dead and I heard Ron sobbing on the other end. Moments later, when he finally spoke, we cried together. When we both gained control, Ron explained to me that the chances that UNC would take Jane were almost nonexistent. The loneliness and despair that I felt as I hung up and wandered back to Jane's room was one of those times when I knew God picked me up and left only one pair of footprints in the sand.

But as I turned the corner toward the nurses' station, Jane's nurse dashed around the counter and rushed toward me. "Mr. Crayton, they're going to take her."

Stunned, I cried, "Carolina?"

"Yes. They want us to fly her up there right away."

"For a heart transplant?" I raised my hands toward heaven.

"Yes, they said that since she'd been on the liver transplant list that she met all the criteria. They've already placed her on the list."

"I've got to tell the others!" I shouted. "Thank you, God."

As I burst into the room, my brother Frank and his wife Dana had joined Debby, Peggy and Powell. My good news was met by shocked silence. None of us had more than a thread of hope that this would have ever happened. We all knew that even now Jane was in critical condition and we'd been informed that she might not even make the trip to Chapel Hill. Once again we let hope back into our lives and the roller coaster could try once more to climb to the top.

"Oh my God," I said. "I've got to call Ron. If they come to get Jane before I get back, someone come and get me. I'll be in the stairwell."

I borrowed my brother's cell phone and dashed for the stairwell. As I ran, I thanked God over and over for the miracle he'd just given me. Years ago I learned that miracles come in all sizes—not just the ones where, for no expandable reason, an illness goes away or a cripple all of a sudden walks again. And I knew that they were all connected.

Ron must have told his receptionist that I might call as she put me right through. When I finished telling Ron what had happened, as before, there was a deafening silence on his end. When he finally did answer, the first words I heard were "Praise God. Skip, ever since we talked, I couldn't find the strength to go back to work. I've been standing here in my office staring out the window and praying. Oh, my God, Skip, he's answered my prayers. God has given us a miracle."

"Yes, Ron." I wiped my eyes. "We have another chance. Just pray that she makes it there." A tap on my shoulder told me I had to hang up. "The helicopter crew is ready, Ron. I've got to go. I'll call you when I know more. Goodbye."

"Keep me in the loop," were the last words I heard as I flipped the cell phone off.

When I reached Jane's room, the flight crew had already transferred her to the gurney. I had no idea whether or not she had been alert enough to feel my arms as I placed them around her, or my kiss on her forehead, or to understand me when I told her that I loved her. But I know that love binds two hearts together and I am sure that through that, because of that bond we'd shared from the first day I laid eyes on her in the seventh grade, that somehow she knew.

Before the flight crew took Jane, I covered her with the little down comforter that Dana had given her, a blanket that had kept her warm so many nights. "Please make sure this gets to Chapel Hill with her," I said. "It'll make her feel safe and warm."

And once more we prayed. Holding hands, we circled around Jane as Powell led us in prayer. Then it was time to let go and once again watch as someone took my precious Jane, the very person I loved most in the world on what would be a journey of life or death.

Chapter 26

*T*HE FIVE OF US stood silently, following the helicopter as it flew off into the clear western sky. Not until the dot disappeared did we leave the parking lot to make the hour-long trip back to New Bern. What had begun as a promising day had deteriorated into darkness, yet had ended with a tiny ray of hope. *How quickly things can change,* I thought. Now we had to get home and pack for a prolonged stay. I had to make arrangements for Little Mutt, and Debby had to do the same for her daughter. I never asked the question, I knew my angel sister would be there to hold my hand once again.

Peggy stayed to help us get ready to leave. It was well after dark when we pulled out of my driveway and started our journey west. The darkness, combined with the similarities to the last time I'd had to follow Jane to Chapel Hill, made this trip strangely different. Instead of the constant ringing of a cell phone and the sound of country music on the radio, this time the only sound was the rumble of the tires. Even the light from the silent radio cast an eerie green light around the cabin of the car.

About halfway into our trip, the silence shattered. My cell rang. It was Jane's cousin Phyllis who lived in nearby Raleigh. "Skip, I heard about Jane," she said. "I'm at the hospital. I'll be there until you get here."

"Is she...? Is she...? Phyllis, did she make it?" I held back the tears almost afraid of her answer.

"She's in the Cardiac Care Unit on the second floor of the women's hospital."

"Thank God," I prayed. "Did you see her?"

"For just a moment. She was asleep."

"We'll be there in about two hours. We're coming straight to the hospital."

"I'll be in the waiting room. Is there anything else I can do?"

"God bless you, Phyllis. You're doing it." I said as I hung up.

Like the ocean on a windless day, calmness swept over me. Just knowing that she'd gotten there was a huge relief. I was glad that Phyllis was there. If Jane died before we got there, at least she would not be alone.

As we continued westward, a strange thought spread before me. Jane and Phyllis had grown up together in the same town with less than a year separating them. Actually, they'd grown up more like sisters and, for the most part throughout their younger years, there had never been a sense of competition between them. Even so, as they got older, they drifted apart. I'm sure the physical distance probably played a part, but I'd always suspected some unresolved issue. Then one day, as if the sun had risen in the West, Jane made up her mind to reconcile and renew their friendship. Whatever had put the gulf between them, Jane had made it her mission to resolve the differences. She put fault or blame completely out of the picture. To Jane, rebuilding that closeness was all that mattered to her. And just recently, Jane had done the same thing with two other friends, mending broken fences and rebuilding friendships once lost.

As I sat there in the darkness as Debby drove us westward, my mind drifted back to that afternoon at the beach when Jane told me that she was going to die. Could those reconciliations have been a part of something she knew was going to be inevitable? Could it have been her conscience cleansing itself in an effort to help Jane put her things in order before she died? If that was the case, no doctor or hospital in the world would ever be able to change things. I shuddered and quickly found a hiding place in my mind for such thoughts. If God was going to give us another miracle, I had to send out positive energy. I was not ready to give up hope. Jane had gotten to Chapel Hill alive, and I knew she was going to make it. I assured myself that, together, we were going to ride that roller coaster to the top.

Chapter
27

I LOOKED AT MY WATCH as we pulled into the empty parking lot in front of the hospital. It was just past 10:00 p.m. It was all so strange. Only weeks before, Jane had been given her walking papers. For all purposes, she was cured. Yet, here we were again. My footsteps echoed off the marble floor and bounced across the walls of a lobby whose only inhabitant was an employee sitting half-awake at the information desk.

As we walked past the perpetual motion machine on the way to the elevators, a part of me wanted to curse its very existence. That thought quickly gave way to thanking God that I was able to see it again.

When the elevator opened on the second floor, we turned left and walked through double doors. Just inside, we found the waiting room with Phyllis curled up on a chair in the corner. The comfort of seeing her there felt like a fire on a fall day; warm and friendly. When she saw me, she sprang from her seat, rushed over to me and wrapped her arms around me.

"Have you been back in?" I asked.

"No. I called back there a few minutes ago and they said there had been no change. It's just so terrible." Phyllis wiped a tear from her eyes. "Just last week, mom had told me that Jane was going to be okay. What happened?"

119

"It's her heart." I took her hand in mine. "They say she picked up some kind of virus last week and it has damaged her heart beyond repair. If they can get her stable enough, they want to do a heart transplant."

"Would they also do a liver transplant?" she asked.

For the first time in what had seemed like a year, the thought of a liver transplant had never occurred to me. "I don't know. Is it possible to do two at the same time? I just don't know. There's so much to ask."

I looked around the room and saw Debby moving toward the door. "I've got to see her if I can. Phyllis, thanks so much for being here. Knowing you were here really eased my mind," I said as I walked toward the door. "Will you be here much longer?"

Phyllis reached next to the chair and grabbed her bag. "You might be in there a while so I think I'll head home. Call me if anything changes or if there is anything that I can do."

"You're a Godsend," I said as we walked into the hallway that would lead Phyllis to the elevators and Debby and me to the doors that led into the Cardiac Care Unit.

Debby picked up the phone outside the unit's two doors and announced our presence. With a loud click, the automatic doors swung open and we walked into the unit. We checked in at the nurses' station and asked for Jane's room.

"Just over there." The nurse pointed to a room at the far end much like the ones in IMC, enclosed yet surrounded by glass. As we entered, a small light over the sink competed with the orange and green lights emitted by the company of diagnostic machines that carried Jane's vital signs.

Jane was asleep, her down-filled blanket that had accompanied her on her trip, laid neatly atop the ones the hospital had supplied. Debby quickly went to the far side of the bed as I leaned over and kissed my bride on the forehead. For a moment Jane's eyes opened and she smiled. As I looked into her eyes, I knew that she knew we were there. Within seconds, she drifted back off to sleep. Debby and I sat in the dark, quiet of the room, each holding one of Jane's hands. For an hour or two the only sound was that of Jane's breathing and the occasional beeping of one of the machines. It was well after midnight when Debby and I finally checked into the Chapel Hill Holiday Inn. Déjà vu...all over again.

Chapter 28

*W*HEN I AWOKE the next morning, the sun was already up. Actually, it felt more like coming to the next morning. We'd checked into the Holiday Inn a little after midnight and I never remember my head hitting the bed. Debby was still asleep, a little ball curled up in the bed next to me. Quietly, I slipped from the covers and went into the bathroom. Craving a cup of coffee, I found a Mr. Coffee with everything I needed to make a small pot. After starting the coffee, I stepped into the shower and let the hot water flow across the top of my head, hoping it would wash away the cobwebs I'd collected during the hard-slept night. When I got out of the shower, Debby was already up.

"Can this all be a dream?" I asked her. "It seems like we just went through all of this. Can it really be three years later?"

My sister shook her head as she wiped her eyes with a washcloth. Avoiding my question-slash-statement, she asked, "What time is it?"

"A little after seven," I said. "Can you be ready in a half-hour?"

"Fifteen minutes is okay with me." She tossed the washcloth in the sink. "That thing make tea? God, I need a cup."

By eight o'clock, we'd turned off of Highway Fifteen-Five-Oh-One onto Manning Drive and in another five minutes, we'd turned over Debby's Prius to the valet parkers. "I sure hope they know how to turn it off when they park it," she said, referring to her hybrid car.

Unlike the night before, the hospital was back to its Grand Central Station routine, bustling in all directions. Fortunately, we did not bump into anyone as we made our way past that confounded bouncing ball machine toward the elevators. Once inside the CCU, I was quickly introduced to Dr. Runge, Jane's attending physician.

Dr. Marshall Runge, about five-foot-ten, was a man who appeared to be in his late forties with a head full of curly, slightly-graying hair. His smile and demeanor made him immediately likeable. Unlike Dr. Zacks, who was aloof, distant, and only called people by their last names, Marshall and I began our association on a first name basis. What I would later learn was that this warm compassionate man was also a world-renowned cardiologist and the Chief of Medicine at UNC. Jane's doctor was the number one medical doctor in the entire UNC Hospital's system. I'm sure that having Marshall as her doctor didn't just happen by chance. I will never know who, if anyone, had arranged it, but I thanked God for that man and his team.

In bringing me up to speed, Marshall informed me that in her present condition, Jane was not stable enough for a heart transplant. It was their plan to slowly work her toward that goal, however it would take several days to get her there. I would also learn that the going would be slow and would be measured in baby steps.

"All I want is for you to bring her back to me." Tears welled up in my eyes and my voice trembled.

Marshall placed his hand on my shoulder and looked into my eyes. "It's okay, Skip. We've had patients in

123

here in a lot worse condition than your wife, and they literally walked out of here. We're going to do all we can to make that happen for Jane."

"But her liver," I wiped my eyes. "Would you do two transplants at the same time and what are the odds of getting two matches at the same time?" Confusion settled over me like a fog drifting in off the ocean.

"Skip, a double transplant has never been done and I don't see how we'd ever risk that. But her liver is in much better shape than it was three years ago and it is in one heck of a lot better shape than her heart. When the time comes, we'll bring Dr. Zacks back in for his advice."

After a few more questions about Jane and an assurance that I could talk with him at any time, Marshall left the room and our day-long vigil began. Neither Debby nor I had planned to leave Jane alone in the room during the day. And, as that first day wore on, we watched Jane become more aware of her surroundings. By late that afternoon, she had become aware that Debby and I were with her.

Then, just as the doctors were making their evening rounds, I looked up and saw Beverly Perdue walk into the room, followed by her husband Bob Eaves. Instead of the grand entrance she'd made three years before, Beverly walked passed me, touched my shoulder and sat down next to Jane on the edge of her bed. Recognizing her good friend, Jane smiled. It was the first time I'd seen her face light up in more than five days.

After she'd completed her visit and after I'd introduced the lieutenant governor and her husband to Jane's doctors and nurses, Beverly called me out into the hall. "Where are you staying?" she asked.

"The Holiday Inn," I answered.

"Not anymore," she said. "Bob and I want you and Debby to stay with us."

Bob, who had lived in Chapel Hill before they'd married, still owned a house there. Although their primary residence was in New Bern, when the legislature was in session, Bev and Bob stayed at the house in Chapel Hill.

"That's so sweet," I said, "but we can't. That would be too much on you. Heck, we don't know how long we're going to be up here. It could be a month or more."

"Skip Crayton—" Bev spread her feet apart and placed her hands on her waist, and I immediately knew that this would not be an argument I would win. "I am not going to take no for an answer. Anyway, we've got plenty of room and Bob and I probably won't be around for more than four or five days. My schedule calls for me to be in Atlanta, Asheville, and back in New Bern. Here's Bob's cell phone number."

She handed me a piece of paper with the number already on it. I knew that any more protest would get me nowhere; neither she nor Bob would settle for anything else.

"Call Bob when you leave the hospital and he'll meet you and show you the way to the house. We'll talk later."

Beverly grabbed Bob's arm and, almost as quickly as they'd appeared, they crossed the hallway and disappeared through the CCU doors.

I watched Marshall's eyes follow their departure. When they'd gone he turned to me, scratched his head. "Gosh, you know some pretty important people."

"Not really," I smiled. "I know some pretty wonderful people."

Chapter
29

*A*S USUAL, Beverly was right. Once I had placed my pride aside and accepted her invitation, I knew that it had been the right thing for both Debby and me. The house was large enough for us both to have our own bedroom. Because Beverly and Bob were gone most of the time, we basically had the run of the house. Past hospital experiences had taught us to be at the hospital as early as possible and to stay until after the doctors had made evening rounds. We'd found that the full days of caring for Jane not only wore her out, but had the same effect on my sister and me. Some quiet time and a good night's rest did more to charge our batteries than anything else. As the days wore on, staying at Bob's house was just the medicine that Debby and I needed.

Bob Eaves' pride and joy is his rose garden. Roses of all variety and color encircle his patio, filling the air with the fresh fragrance that is rarely surpassed by any other flower. Sitting on that patio with a glass of wine, surrounded by the bouquet and color of Bob's roses, coupled by a growing twilight had a healing effect on me that raised me up and allowed me to face another day.

For the first few days, Jane became more and more aware of her surroundings and by the weekend, we were actually able to communicate with each other. On Saturday, Powell came by for a visit. This wonderful man had been with us from the beginning; at New Bern, in Greenville, and now at Chapel Hill. He and Jane prayed together and talked. From time to time she cried, then just as quickly, she'd break into a smile. It was as if she was in some child-like spell, yet I knew she was aware of those around her. At times she would even take part in conversation. That afternoon, Jimmy came up, spent some time with Jane and spent the night with us at Bob's house.

On Sunday afternoon, Frank brought our mother to see Jane. The second she entered the room, Jane's eyes brightened and she broke into a huge grin. She recognized my mother and was truly excited to see her.

That night, as Debby and I left the hospital, I felt a sense of wellbeing. For the first time in our ordeal, I really believed that Jane was going to come back to me. As we passed the bouncing balls in the lobby, I smiled and looked over at the machine. *We'll be leaving you soon,* I thought. *Then you can ping and bang on someone else's nerves.*

The next day those hopes were dashed. When we entered Jane's room, things were different. More despondent than the day before, she barely recognized me. After giving her a kiss on the forehead, I quickly made my way to the nurses' station.

"What's happened?" I pleaded. "She's different."

"I'm sorry, Mr. Crayton," the nurse said. "I didn't see you come in. Let me call Dr. Runge. He'll be able to explain everything."

I went back to Jane's room, sat down, grabbed her hand and began stroking her arm. Jane tried a faint smile. Marshall must have been nearby as he seemed to have appeared out of nowhere.

"Skip, we've had a little setback."

"What?" I begged.

"You remember the blood clots in her heart?" He came over and sat down next to me.

127

I nodded.

"Well, we think one of them has broken away and that Jane has suffered a mild stroke. We won't know any more until the neurologists have had a chance to look at her. They're making their rounds right now and should be by very shortly."

My heart took a nosedive and crashed onto the floor, followed by that roller coaster car we'd been riding in for so long. For a moment I just sat in silence. I couldn't get the word "suffered" out of my mind. My baby had suffered so much. "Oh God," I prayed. "Things looked so good yesterday. I just knew she'd get better. Now, I'm afraid to ask what's next. What are we going to do?"

An hour later, the neurologists confirmed our fears, but there was some good news. Of all the places a person could have had a stroke, the one Jane had suffered was in the safest place in her brain. Other than a drooping left eye, once the cardiologists had her back on her feet, they expected that she'd fully recover from the stroke. When I heard the news, I thanked God as I heard the clicking sound that started the roller coaster back up the hill. There was still hope.

Chapter 30

*J*ANE'S BRAIN TRUST had just been enlarged as Peggy's ex-husband Frank Tew had joined the team of Cardiologists. Frank, an affable man with an olive complexion and thinning hair, had spent most of his professional years working in Florida. When he retired, he returned to his home state and became an advisor to the Cardiology Department at his alma mater. Having him onboard was like having a family member as part of the team. I had known Frank for more than thirty years and having him around vastly increased my comfort level.

The next day that brain trust increased again. Ron Moore had rearranged his schedule and had come up to see Jane. Ron walked into Jane's room, shook my hand and walked over to Jane's bed. He had not yet had a chance to even look at her chart when he immediately glanced back at me. "Skip, I think she's had a stroke."

I guess that's why I have so much respect for Ron's ability as a doctor. He knew right away something that had taken the neurologists much more time to confirm. But, again, Ron was Jane's primary care physician and he knew her.

"Yes," I answered. "But I'm told it is in as good a place as it could be in."

Before Ron could answer, Frank came into the room. As I started to introduce them, both broke into huge

129

smiles. It seems that they'd known each other in medical school.

It was Ron who actually told me about Marshall. Before then, to me he was just another compassionate UNC doctor. We'd taken a break for lunch in the cafeteria when Ron asked, "How the hell did you get Dr. Runge as Jane's attending physician?"

I reacted with a standard puppy-dog look, cocking my head to one side. "I don't know. Why?"

"He's just about the best doctor here at Chapel Hill." Ron leaned forward and looked me in the eyes. "You didn't know that he is the Chief of Medicine?"

"That's good?"

"She can't get better care."

We finished lunch and returned to the Cardiac Care Unit. As we walked into Jane's room, Debby dozed in a chair next to Jane's bed. Seconds later, Marshall and his staff, along with Frank, followed us into the room.

"Dr. Zacks should be here any minute," Marshall informed us.

When Steven Zacks walks, there is a fluid motion about him as if he were on ice skates. A Canadian, whose only interest other than medicine was ice hockey, may have had something to do with the way he moved. As the automatic doors to the CCU opened, he flowed through them—all five feet of him—his long white coat floating behind him like a cape. It has been said that the only way you can tell that a civil engineer is paying attention to what you're saying is if he is looking at your shoes instead of his. That same type of eye contact would normally describe Dr. Zacks, yet this time as he entered the room, he looked directly at me.

What we learned from Dr. Zacks was that although Jane's liver would probably never fully recover, he felt that it would more than likely withstand a heart transplant. He told us that Jane had been one of his best patients and that her progress had amazed even him.

I shook my head, "She's had a great doctor."

"I really didn't do that much," he said, purposely trying to duck the compliment.

It quickly became apparent to me that this man, whom others called *Little Napoleon* behind his back, was extremely uncomfortable accepting compliments in front of his peers, especially in front of Marshall, his boss.

Like a junkyard dog, I refused to let go and sent the compliment right back. "You sell yourself short, Dr. Zacks. You brought my girl back to me. I'll never forget you for that. Now we need another miracle."

"Mr. Crayton," he glanced around the room at the others, then back at me like a cornered animal looking for a way out, trapped by the admiring looks directed at him by the other doctors. "You give me too much credit."

Out of the corner of my eye I caught Frank's widening grin. He seemed to really enjoy the banter between the doctor and me and the fact that I refused to let him back away from the compliment I knew he so richly deserved.

Without further comment, Dr. Zacks looked over at Marshall. "It could be difficult, but in Mrs. Crayton's case, it is definitely doable."

"Thanks, Steven," Marshall smiled and looked at me. "Looks like we have our answer. I just hope that we can live up to the job you've done."

Accepting that compliment from the Chief of Medicine was difficult at best for this private-dedicated man. As hard as it was for him to reveal, I already knew Dr. Zacks' heart was in the right place. It was the hint of blush that grazed his cheeks that revealed his true compassion to the rest of those in the room.

After Dr. Zacks left, I sat by and marveled at what took place next. Marshall, his chief Fellow, along with Frank and Ron spent the next fifteen minutes discussing Jane's condition, her prognosis and what they felt was needed to get her to that point where a successful heart transplant could take place. As I followed the discussion, it became immediately apparent to me that Ron's presence was acknowledged, not as a bystander, but as a colleague. His opinion and comments quickly convinced the team that he knew what he was talking about. It was as if he'd taken control as I followed the nods of approval his suggestion had made. When the conversation had ended, a plan of attack had been placed into action. And again I heard the click of the roller coaster.

As the hospital doctors left the room, Frank called me out into the hall. "Did you understand all that?" he asked.

"I think so," I answered. "What I heard was that ya'll have agreed on what you have to do next and how it's to be done."

"Yeah, that's true, but did you realize that Ron Moore is probably one of the smartest doctor I've ever seen? He is as up-to-speed as the best cardiologist here on staff. Man, I'm impressed. Listening to his comments and what he had to add was like Jesus teaching the Rabbis. This guy is for real. I don't think there is a better team of doctors anywhere in the country than the ones looking after Jane, and that includes Ron Moore."

Chapter
31

*G*IVING UP is something that I've always had a hard time doing. To me the glass is always half-full. As long as there is even a tiny sliver of hope, there is a chance that the glass will not just fill up, it will overflow.

The next morning as we passed through the doors that lead to the CCU, I noticed a much more distant look in the eyes of the nurses.

Jane smiled at me as I entered the room. Before I could get over to her bed she drifted back off to sleep. It seemed that just knowing that Debby and I were close by gave her the peace to rest. As I stood by her bed stroking her hair, I wondered what she dreamt about. I knew she realized how sick she was. There were times during her waking moments she would tell me that she was going to die. She even mentioned that she'd seen people who'd already passed on. The names of one father and his son who had died some years before came up over and over. Although Jane knew them both, she did not know them well. I never understood why the names came up, but to hear her, it was as if one or both had visited with her during the night. Debby and I assured her that the doctors were going to make her just fine and that soon she'd be coming home. I never felt like she believed me.

As Jane drifted back off to sleep, her nurse came into the room. "What's wrong?" I asked.

She glanced away then back at me. "Nothing."

"Nothing?" I asked.

"No, not really," she answered as she busied herself checking the wires and monitors that conveyed Jane's vital signs to the machines in her room and repeated them to similar ones at the nearby nurses' station. "But I do have a question. The doctors wanted to know if you knew whether or not the central IV had been placed in Jane's neck by a doctor or by someone else, like an EMT."

The IV she referred to was a multi-port device that was plugged into Jane's jugular vein in her neck. It not only allowed for fluids to be injected, it also allowed for them to be withdrawn. Jane's veins had become so fragile that it had become almost impossible to insert a standard IV anywhere else.

"Sure," I wrinkled my brow. "It was put in by either a surgeon or radiologist back at Craven. Why do you want to know?"

"The doctors were just wondering, is all," she said as she continued to fuss about Jane.

Moments later, one of Jane's doctors came in and asked me the same question. That's when I got the answer to the sullen mood that hung over the CCU.

"What's this all about?" I asked the doctor.

"We found some infection. Her white count is up and we were not sure where it is coming from. Sometimes, when central IVs are inserted in less-than-sterile conditions—like in the back of an ambulance—they can be the source for the infection. I'm afraid in this case we'll probably rule that one out." The doctor shook his head, walked over to Jane and toyed with the IV.

"You got any other idea what may be causing the infection?" The rational part of me asked the question,

134

but the part of me that holds on to dreams and hopes did not want to hear the answer; fearing the worst.

The doctor walked over to me, placed his hand on my shoulder and softly said, "I'm afraid it might be pneumonia."

I closed my eyes. My little voice had warned me that that dreaded word might come out. My heart crashed once again onto the floor, but this time it would be too damaged to get back up. I felt empty, naked, and afraid.

I've never studied people's eyes much. I think I've spent most of my life listening or watching body language. But during that time at CCU, I learned that the eyes can speak louder than any voice. And they always speak the truth. Before the doctor left, he placed his assuring hand on my arm, but as he spoke words of hope, his eyes told me that this would probably be the beginning of the end.

After he left, I told Debby that I'd need to make a few phone calls, so I left to go outside. What I really wanted was some time alone. I had to deal with the fact that, barring a miracle, Jane would not come back to me, that she was going to die.

As I waited for the elevator, I prayed to God for one more miracle. I asked Him to forgive me for asking for another miracle, yet I prayed that He would send her back to me one more time. I promised God that I would do anything if only He'd give her back.

That's when a bell, louder than any I'd ever heard in my life, clanged in my head. I realized that I was praying for the wrong thing. At the time, I had a friend whose wife had been in a coma for more than five years, somewhere in some sort of suspended animation between heaven and earth; still clinically alive. Jane had made me promise over and over that I would not allow that to happen to her. She did not want to live without life. She wanted to be allowed to die and move on to heaven.

135

"Oh God," I prayed. "Please forgive me. Please, please ignore what I just asked for. It was such a selfish prayer. I only pray, dear God, that *Your* will be done, not mine."

Sometimes when we pray, we get answers that we really don't want. As I leaned against the wall waiting for the elevator, a sense of peace flowed throughout me like baptismal waters. Sure, I was still afraid. I hurt beyond all measure, but I knew right then that for Jane and for me, God had a plan for us both and that I had to trust in Him. Whatever the outcome, I knew that He was in charge and that He would see me through the darkness. I knew He'd reach down and carry me, just as he'd done so many other times in my life.

Chapter 32

*E*VEN KNOWING that God was with me, the idea that I'd lose my precious Jane made my life almost unbearable. The next few days were filled with a sense of hopelessness and despair. In the Gulf of Mexico, Hurricane Katrina took aim at New Orleans, the news reports only amplified my feeling of impending doom. Each evening as I left the hospital, I died a little more inside.

Then late one evening, about two days later, the call I'd dreaded came. I felt numb and despondent as Debby and I left for the hospital. Inside, I knew that it would be for the last time, yet hope still hung around me like the fragrance of Bob's roses.

CCU was morgue-like quiet as my sister and I entered. The nurses, compassionate beyond all expectation, hugged us and led us into the room. All the tubes and hoses had been removed, only the heart monitor remained. Jane looked angelic as she slept, awaiting for God to come to her. For the next three hours, Debby and I held her hand and prayed. Along with the hospital chaplain, we sang hymns and prayed some more.

The curtains had been drawn around Jane's bed giving an almost tomb-like appearance, yet there was no feeling of gloom. I've never really understood angels. The Bible doesn't talk about them much, but I've been told that they are real, but not human; that they are messengers from God, our protectors. All my life I've wanted there to be angels, but I have doubted their existence, let alone their presence. But that night in Jane's room as she lay dying, I felt surrounded by love. I knew that there were angels among us.

Jane's breathing slowed. For the first time in almost three weeks, her heart rate had returned to normal. Her eyes remained closed, yet I knew that she knew I was with her. As she struggled to take her last breaths, I told Jane how much I loved her and that I knew that I would see her again. Just before 4:00 a.m., she squeezed my hand one last time and passed into God's hands. Forty-three years of loving the most precious person in the world had just ended. And I thought my life had ended, too.

PART THREE

"The second Jane died, I knew there would
be life after death for her, but I never thought
there'd be life after her death for me."

Chapter
33

*J*UST LIKE THE DARKNESS that engulfed the world the afternoon of the Crucifixion, a black fog descended upon me as my sister and I walked to the elevators. The ride to the first floor was so quiet I heard the cables creaking and snapping as they lowered the car past each floor. Unlike the Grand Central Station-like bustle we'd experienced when we'd left the hospital three years before, this time, the lobby reflected our mood. And much like the time my sister and I had first entered the building, the vast lobby was vacant except for the person dozing at the information desk. The only sound came from the perpetual motion machine; its balls pinging and whirring even louder than before.

Before I left the lobby, I turned and glared back at that annoying machine. "I hope you bring joy or amusement to some young person," I whispered as if it was able to hear me. "But I pray I'll never have to see you again."

I caught up with Debby in the parking lot, a cigarette in one hand, the other clutching the back of her neck as she walked aimlessly around the car. For a moment I followed her as we circled like two birds, trying to find a place to land.

Finally, Debby stopped, turned, and fell into my arms. I don't remember how long we stood in that

141

parking lot holding on to each other, but when we let go I felt as if I didn't know where I was. Around me, the setting was so familiar that at any other time I could have drawn a map with my eyes closed. But right then, I didn't recognize a single object. I'd never felt so lost in all my life.

Off toward the east, I noticed the sky start to lighten, almost beckoning me home. I may have felt lost, but I knew where I had to go. Other than to head back home, I had no clue what to do next. I wiped my eyes and looked at my sister. "I guess we have to make some calls."

"Yeah," Debby said as she stepped on her smoke. "We probably need to call Frank first."

My brother is the most pragmatic person I know. When solving a problem, I've always charged right in the front door. Frank, on the other hand, has always approached a problem from the back door. Even though our methods were usually at opposite ends, we nearly always came up with the same results. He is very family-oriented, and he and his wife Dana are two of the best parents I know. Although very private with his emotions, Frank's compassion is limitless.

"Hello," he said. When he answered the phone, I could visualize my brother wiping the sleep from his eyes.

I took a deep breath. I never realized how difficult it would be to tell someone I loved that she'd passed. At first I couldn't speak.

"Hello," my brother said again.

This time all I could do was to clear my throat.

"Skip. Is that you?"

"Yeah. It's me." A long pause followed. In the background, I heard Frank's wife asking if it was me, followed a whispered. "Oh no."

"Frank," I finally said. "Jane just died."

142

That is all I remember about that conversation other than Frank telling Debby and me to go back to Bob's house and to not drive home.

"Stay right where you are," he said. "We're coming to get you." Three hours later and after ten or fifteen additional phone calls, I was in Debby's car with my brother and Debby was with Dana, heading home.

Chapter
34

*T*HE DRIVE BACK to New Bern that morning passed quickly. My phone rang constantly, but I answered only a few of the calls. We'd all decided not to tell anyone other than very close friends and family about Jane's death until Debby could tell her daughter Jenna. We didn't want Jenna to find out from someone else. My caller ID told me that somehow the word had gotten out. What I didn't know was that my mother had all but broadcasted it over the television. Fortunately, Debby got to Jenna before she'd heard anything.

I desperately wanted to get home. I knew that Jane would never come home to me again, but I'd been away for so long and I needed the womb-like setting of my home and my bed. And I needed to see Little Mutt. Now, she was the closest living thing in my immediate family that connected me to Jane.

Little Mutt had never spent the night by herself. She'd never stayed in a kennel. A wonderful woman named Rosa, God bless her soul, had stayed with her each night during the three weeks I'd been away. Along with Rosa, my wonderful friends Jimmy and Patti, and Bill and Dorrie Benners had helped to take care of my little girl.

My heart stopped when we pulled into my driveway. Before me lay the house that I'd designed and built for

Jane; the house that she and I had made into a home. A home so full of memories, a place that would never again hear her laughter or feel her touch or smell the wonderful aromas of food that she'd so lovingly prepared. Even the lingering fragrance of her perfume would soon disappear. It wasn't a home anymore. Now, it was only a house—one that I would have to learn to live in alone. A chill swept over me like a March northeaster, and once again I cried. God, I missed her so much.

Frank stopped the car and I got out. The summer had been so hot and I'd wished for an early fall. Sometime during the last few days I'd gotten my wish. The morning was bright and cool. Bill and Dorrie, and Jimmy and Patti along with Annie Parker had been sitting on the deck waiting for us. The hugs from my good friends momentarily dissolved the chill and sent loving warmth throughout me like a child being tucked in by his mother on a cold winter night. For a time, we stood together and cried. Nothing had to be said, just the touch and compassion of loved ones was all I wanted at the time.

Strengthened by their love, I looked around. "Where's Little Mutt?"

"She's inside," Patti cautioned. "Just be patient with her. Skip, you've been gone a long time, and I don't know how she'll react. She's really taken to all of us. She might not even remember you. Please, just give her a little time."

"Thanks, Patti," I smiled and said. "Let's let her be the judge of that."

"Okay." Patti shrugged and walked to the back door and opened it. Little Mutt peeped out of the door and slowly walked onto the deck.

"Where's my Little Mutt?" I shouted.

Before I could get the words out it was as if someone had shot her out of a cannon. She jumped into high

145

gear and raced across the deck toward me. As Little Mutt got to within ten feet of me, she became airborne and leapt into my arms—licking me for all she was worth.

As Little Mutt literally washed my face with her tongue, I glanced over at Patti. "I believe she remembers me." It was the first time I'd smiled in days.

Chapter
35

*W*E ALL TEND to take good friends for granted. It's like they're always there, especially in good times. These are the folks we choose to share our lives with. They are the first ones we call when our kid makes the dean's list. Or the ones we can't wait to show off our new car, or the ones with whom we plan a trip or celebrate a birthday. They're the ones we talk to every day and have dinner with a couple of times a month. Just like family, Christmas would not be Christmas without them. They share our joy. And they also share our sorrow. It is then that they become more than just friends, they become family.

The minute Little Mutt and I walked into the house, my friends took over my life. And I let them. I guess I learned a lot when Jimmy's first wife, Louise, died. Jimmy is, and has always been, a controller, from the time that we were kids back in the old neighborhood until now. But when Louise died, he handed the wheel over to Jane and me and we helped to lead Jimmy and his family through those rough days and into the future. It has always seemed so strange that Jimmy and I, closer than brothers, would suffer the same fate—losing a wife. What Jane and I did for Jimmy was about to come back to me tenfold. He and Patti took over my life.

147

For the next hour or so, most of my time was spent fielding phone calls from friends and acquaintances. Just before lunch, Patti came up to me and placed her hand on my shoulder. "Skip, you've been up all night. The next few days are going to be really draining. Why don't you and Little Mutt go upstairs and take a nap?"

"Patti, there's so much to do," I protested. "I've got to get hold of Powell and the funeral home and the cemetery—"

"Powell's coming over at four. Frank talked with the funeral home and has that set up for tomorrow morning. After that, he'll take you to pick out the cemetery." Patti reached down, picked up Little Mutt and handed her to me. "You go get some rest. We'll look after everything else."

I knew she was right. Fatigue worsened the numbness I felt and would probably affect my judgment. I took her advice, went upstairs and placed my shadow in the bed next to me. I was afraid I wouldn't be able to fall asleep. Jane's memory surrounded me. The bed felt like her, and I could even smell her. I closed my eyes. At least I could have some quiet time with my thoughts. The next thing I remembered was Jimmy waking me to let me know that Powell was downstairs. I had slept soundly for almost five hours with no dreams.

The meeting with Powell lasted about an hour. Because the Labor Day weekend had just started, we decided to hold Jane's service on Monday at 11:00 a.m. Since Jane had made me promise not to have an open casket, we decided to have the visitation on Sunday night at the house.

Along with the preparations for the funeral, I told Powell that I wanted the songs *Here am I Lord* and *Let There be Peace on Earth* to be sung by the congregation. I also asked him if he would contact my friend Chantal Hollatschek and ask her if she would sing *Standing on*

Holy Ground. Standing on Holy Ground was Jane's favorite praise song. It had been sung at my father's funeral as well as Jane's mom's. And Chantal was Jane's favorite singer. For her to sing that song at Jane's funeral would bring a smile down from Heaven.

Powell sat across from me in the family room. Little Mutt snuggled patiently in my lap as we discussed the details of Jane's service. Just before Powell left, he asked if I had any more questions.

"Yes," I said. "There's one more very important question I have to ask." I reached over and patted Little Mutt on the head. "Powell, I've got one more request."

"Sure, Skip," he answered, a queried look on his face.

"You know that since Jane and I don't have any children, our dogs have been our family. I was wondering if I could bring Little Mutt with me and let her sit in my lap during the service. It would mean so much to me, and I know it would mean so much to Jane.

Without missing a beat, Powell replied, "Gosh, I've never been asked that before, but sure. You can bring Little Mutt with you. I can't imagine anything more fitting."

I smiled and again tears welled up in my eyes. "Thank you."

Chapter
36

*T*HAT NIGHT I'd never felt so much love around me. My friends comforted me and helped me to release some of my sorrow. I hurt but I never felt alone. I guess my friends understood more than I did how lonely the house could be. That first night, my very close friends Bob and Missy Baskerville came in from Oriental and stayed the night with me. They are old and dear friends with whom I'd probably sailed half a million miles. Having them with me that night gave me the security I'd learned to depend on during our years of racing sailboats. I knew that while they were on watch, I'd be safe.

Little Mutt became my shadow, at my feet and side. I knew somehow that she knew what was going on. She had always been a very active little dog; chasing her tail, bounding to the door at walk time and devouring her food. Just the sound of my voice caused her tail to tick tock behind her. Now, she rarely wagged it, keeping it tucked between her legs. She appeared to be mourning deeply. The rare times when I had to leave her, she parked herself in a corner, her head between her paws, looking more like a dust mop than a dog. Yes, she knew. I'll never know how, but she knew that Jane was never coming back.

It was late when Little Mutt and I climbed the stairs that first night. When I got into bed, she curled next to my feet as I pulled the covers over my head and said my prayers. Reaching over to Jane's side of the bed, I prayed that it had all been a bad dream. The place where she'd slept for more than thirty years, now empty, felt cold. I missed her more than I thought I could bare, and I desperately wanted her back. Gathering her pillow close to my face, I caught a whiff of her perfume. I clutched that pillow tightly, holding on to one last part of Jane. I knew I'd never see her again, nor hear her laugh or feel her touch. I knew I'd never again taste her lips, but for one brief fleeting moment as I smothered my face into that pillow, I held her for one last time. I never remembered falling asleep.

The next thing I knew was Jimmy knocking on my bedroom door. "You awake," he called through the door.

I wiped the crumbs from my eyes as Little Mutt stretched at the end of the bed. "Yeah," I answered. "What time is it?"

"A little after nine," he said. "Come on down. Coffee's on."

"Okay."

I reached over, pulled Little Mutt to my face, gave her a kiss, and placed her down on the floor. After I brushed my teeth and threw on a tee-shirt and a pair of shorts, Little Mutt and I went downstairs.

As I walked into the kitchen, Jimmy stood by the sink pouring me a cup of coffee. Through the kitchen window, I could see Bob and Missy sitting at the glass-top table on the deck. "You been here all night?" I asked Jimmy.

"No. I just got back," he said, his back to me as he placed the pot back on the coffeemaker. "Patti will be over shortly. Oh yeah, what time is Frank coming by?"

I'd almost forgotten that this was the morning that we'd be facing the gruesome task of picking out a casket and selecting a crypt along with the other tasks that went along with making funeral arrangements.

Frank and Debby had set up the appointment with the funeral home for 10:30 a.m. and the one at the cemetery for 11:30 a.m. I had been a part of the almost matter-of-fact solemn occasion of planning a funeral more times than I cared to remember, starting with our daughter Mary Ruth, then Jane's sister, both her parents and, finally, my father. It was an experience I'd never wish on anyone even once, let alone five times. But selecting a place to bury Jane would be a first.

I took the coffee, thanked Jimmy and looked at my watch. "Gosh, they'll be here in a half-hour, and I've got to write Jane's obituary to take with us to the funeral home."

Writing an obituary is pretty basic composition. I'd written the one for Jane's mom when she died, and it seemed so easy, listing dates, family members—both dead and alive—and accomplishments, all to announce the passing. For Jane, I wanted to do something more. I wanted to tell of her life. Writing an obituary for Jane was "pure" torture, yet I knew that I could tell of her life better than anyone else. As I sat in my office in front of my computer, it was as if she had placed her hand on my shoulder while I wrote, cried, and wrote some more. When I finally finished, Frank was knocking on the door. I always re-write, even when I'm writing for the newspaper. Heck, my last book, *The Letter Sweater* took twenty re-writes before I felt it was polished enough for publication. As Earnest Hemmingway put it, "first drafts ain't shit." But as I read and re-read that first draft, I could not find any reason to change a single word. I knew somehow Jane would be happy with what I'd written.

Chapter 37

*M*Y FRIEND Roger Smith could just about do anything, especially when it came to building things. Roger also had one of the most unique senses of humor—no, let's call it what it was: one of the hokiest senses of humor that I'd even seen. It was so hokey that he was downright funny. Within minutes of meeting someone, Roger would ask the new acquaintance if they'd like to see a picture of his "pride and joy." When the unsuspecting new friend agreed, Roger would pull out his wallet and fumble with a picture. Expecting a picture of a child or spouse, the expressions of those who saw the photo ranged from a quizzical stare to a belly laugh. What the photograph contained was a picture of a can of "Pride" furniture polish along with a bottle of "Joy" dishwashing liquid.

Roger died a few years ago, and with him went that childlike humor I so enjoyed. But before he died, however, he built a fishpond in our backyard which became Jane's "pride and joy." Jane filled her pond with Koi and Goldfish, each one appropriately named. She loved that pond. It was her most peaceful place, a place where she spent hours, reading her Bible, or just contemplating life.

For me, I hated that fishpond, mostly because it was my job to clean out the pump that fed the waterfall— every day. Imagine thirty-six rather large fish in a pond ten feet wide, twelve feet long and two feet deep, pooping all day long. I'd have to reach into that water, retrieve the pump and clean it out. Because Jane loved that pond, I never complained. Having her back in my life and seeing the pleasure it gave her, cleaning the pump was a small price for me to pay.

One winter morning after reaching into that almost frozen pond, Jane asked the strangest question. "If I had died when I went into that coma, would you have kept the fishpond?"

At the time Jane asked the question, she was on the mend. The thought of her dying was as remote to me as one of my books making the *New York Times'* Best Seller list. I answered that as soon as I'd found a home for the fish, I'd have brought in a dump truck and filled that sucker. We both laughed.

Just before Debby, Frank and I left for the funeral home, my sister noticed that the water in the pond was low so she placed a hose in it to bring the pond back up to normal.

After making all the final arrangements, my brother and sister, and I returned just before noon. The cost of dying isn't cheap. By the time we returned home, I'd spent more than ten thousand dollars. As we drove into the driveway, I discovered Ron Moore on his hands and knees in front of my house planting flowers. Ron knew how much Jane loved flowers and he wanted the entrance to our home to reflect that love. He might have been planting flowers for Jane, but he was also showing his love for me.

As Ron went back to planting his flowers, I entered the house through the front door, something I seldom ever do. Inside, my wonderful friends were busy cleaning the house and fixing all types of food, most of which had been brought in by many of Jane's other friends. As I walked through the kitchen toward the deck, a whirlwind of activity exploded in the back yard.

Bill Benners dashed across the yard toward the pond with a net in his hand and quickly started dipping fish from the pond into a couple of coolers. Bob and Missy stirred the pond and dipped buckets as deep as they would go, bringing up water and dumping it into the coolers. Over by the fence, my sister stood, her head buried in Jimmy's shoulder, crying.

"What's going on?" I shouted as I stepped out onto the deck.

Debby turned to look at me, her eyes red as tears streamed down her cheeks. "I'm so sorry," she sobbed.

Then I saw what all the commotion was about. Floating listlessly at the top of the water was a dozen or so of Jane's fish. My heart plunged and my stomach turned sour.

"No!" I whispered to myself as I dashed to the pond. *God, it was only a joke*, I cried to myself, *please don't let them die, too.*

"I'm so sorry," my sister cried. "I left the water on in the pond and the chlorine is killing all Jane's fish."

"They're not all dead," Bob shouted as he tried to resuscitate a large white Koi. "This one is coming around."

Because of their quick thinking and even quicker action, Bill, Bob, and Missy saved more than half the fish; all now bumping into each other in two large Igloo coolers. By bringing up water from the bottom of the pond and quickly getting the ones still alive out of the water, they'd avoided what at the time would have been complete disaster. I had never really wanted to fill in that fishpond. Abruptly God had reminded me again to watch what I asked for. It might come true. More than ever I now wanted that pond as a memorial to Jane.

Bill looked at me after he'd picked up the last survivor and said, "I guess we'll have to drain the pond."

"No, they sell something at Bill's Pet Shop that will get rid of the chlorine," I said as I walked over to my still weeping sister. "All we have to do is stir it in and wait a few minutes. Then we can put the others back in."

"I'll be right back." Bill said.

As I got to my sister, she was still holding on to Jimmy. I took her in my arms and stroked her hair. "Sweetie, don't cry. It's going to be all right."

"But I killed Jane's fish!"

"No, you didn't. More than half made it and anyway, you were not the only one who forgot about the hose. I am as responsible as you." I placed my hands on her cheeks and gazed directly into her eyes. "Thank you, precious. If you hadn't noticed what was happening, they would have all died. Thanks for saving Jane's fish."

Chapter 38

*T*HE NEXT TWO DAYS buzzed by in a dull numbness that I can only liken to wondering around in a maze. I knew I was going in some direction, but I wasn't sure where I was going. For the most part, I just followed the lead of my friends and family. My cousin Fred Hessick came in from Washington and settled into one of the bedrooms. Separated by a six-hour drive, Fred and I have remained as close as any relative that I have and he surely takes the place on my right hand as one of my five closest friends.

The night before the memorial service, we held the visitation at the house. To my amazement, the steam of well-wishers and those bearing condolences continued, non-stop for almost three hours.

The Crayton family is a small unit, with most of my cousins from the Greensboro area of North Carolina. My father's sister never had any children and his brother only had two boys, Jim and Grey. Although apart, we were a close-knit family and both came with their families.

On my mother's side, other than my Fred, I'd never built more than a couple of long-term relationships. I was surprised when most of my cousins, even one who lives in Tennessee, made the trip to New Bern.

Just like with my family, Jane's family had moved to New Bern after World War Two. Jane's father's sister, Christine, and her family came to New Bern when her husband Johnny opened a business with Jane's dad. Jane was able to grow up with her two cousins, Tim and Phyllis.

Jane's mom was the last sibling of a family with five girls and one boy. When Jane's grandparents abruptly died, her only uncle, a lawyer and later a judge, finished raising the girls, sending each one to college. Only when Jane became sick did she really reach out to that side of her family, rekindling a bond that had always existed, but one that had simmered for many years. To my astonishment, all her cousins, but the one who lived in California, made the services.

Amazements abounded those few days, but what took me most by surprise was the number of people who came to the visitation that I did not know; people who had in some way known Jane or who had been touched by her. As the days passed and I opened the hundreds of cards and letters that would eventually flow into my mailbox, that amazement would overflow as well.

Jane had been very active in a Bible study group that met at Garber Church on Tuesday mornings. Although they met at Garber, the makeup of that group was ecumenical. Nearly every church in New Bern had a representative in that group. The night of the visitation, those women insisted that they be a part of the gathering and they literally took over the house and kitchen, making sure that everyone felt welcome and that there was food and drink for those who wanted to linger and talk with others in attendance.

The outpouring of love that night was overwhelming, yet when it was over, I felt drained. Before Jane's Bible group left, they gathered around the pond, held hands, and prayed. I had already asked them if they would sit together up front as the honorary pallbearers.

After the well-wishers had left, I melted into the couch with Little Mutt in my lap and wept. Surrounding me were my special loved ones; my wonderful close friends whose footprints were there in the sand next to God's as they helped Him carry me through the darkness. After a bite to eat and a couple of glasses of wine, Little Mutt and I slipped upstairs.

The death of a loved one is emotional and exhausting. Even with the help of close friends, the toll is unimaginable until one goes through the experience. Couple that with the ups and downs of hope and despair of a prolonged hospital stay, then add to that finally knowing that the loved one is going to die. Then pile on top of all of that, the waiting for that person to pass into God's hands, the emotional experience and the lack of sleep that accompanies it all. It is no wonder why the numbness sets in.

Yet, as tired as I was that night, as I turned back the covers for Little Mutt and me, I struggled to stay awake a little longer as I held on to the very last whiff of my precious Jane.

Chapter 39

*S*LEEP IS SOMETHING I've never had to battle. Normally, I'm gone within minutes of my head hitting the pillow. Dreams, on the other hand, are something I've struggled with for years. I either do not dream at all or I have extremely vivid ones that leave me exhausted when I awake.

Those dreams generally involve a return home from some distant place. The journey, never easy, is full of roadblocks and handicaps. Instead of just opening a door and crossing a street, my trip involves climbing stairs, going through windows and crossing rickety bridges, going down into basements, crawling through sewer pipes, and balancing along parapet walls just to cover a few feet of ground.

In almost all those dreams, I am responsible for one or both of my dogs, making sure that they don't get away from me, or fall, or drown, or get run over by a car or some menacing machine. When Thumper was alive, he and Little Mutt were a part of those dreams. After his death, Little Mutt became my sole responsibility in my dreams.

The morning of Jane's funeral, I awoke exhausted and, as always when I dream those dreams, I immediately reached down to check on my little girl. Touching her furry head, and feeling her lick my hand, gave me a sigh of relief. As I lay there gathering my wits

160

about me, I remembered that the day to say goodbye to Jane had arrived. But instead of getting up to face it, I pulled the covers over my head and hid in the sanctuary of the bed we'd shared for more than thirty-seven years. I wanted to hide. I prayed that I had not awakened but was just in the middle of one of my strange journey-like dreams. But a knock on my bedroom door jolted me back to the reality I did not want to face.

"Time to get up?" Jimmy said, his voiced muffled by the closed door.

"What time is it?" I pulled the covers down, just enough to uncover my face.

"After eight," he replied. "Some of the family have already started to arrive. You probably need to get up."

The door cracked open and Jimmy peered into the room as I kicked off the covers and swung my legs off the bed onto the floor. "Come on in."

The smell of coffee drifted in before Jimmy had even made it through the door. "Thanks," I said as I took the cup from him. My eyes welled up, as I sipped the cup. "Jimmy, what would I do without you and Patti? How can I ever repay..."

"It's what families do for each other," he placed his hand on my shoulder, "It doesn't have to be repaid. Anyway, you've forgotten all you and Jane did for me when Weezie died."

"But that was different," I protested. "We were fam..." I barely got the "F" out before I caught myself.

Jimmy raised his eyebrows in a "see what I mean" look.

I took a deep breath and sat down in the chair next to my bed. "Jimmy, my brain feels like it's working in slow motion. I'm not sure I know what is going on inside me, let alone around me."

"Skip, I know," he walked to the door. Before he left, he turned back to me and shook his head. "And believe me, what you're feeling will not pass quickly. It will be with you for some time to come. But remember one thing: you will not have to face all this by yourself as long as you trust in God and let your family and friends love you. I can assure you, you cannot do this alone. But with that love, you will get through this and the months yet to come."

Chapter 40

*W*ITH LITTLE MUTT in my arms, I stood in the narthex of the church. As I glanced around, I saw that people had been seated in the choir loft, telling me that the church was full. Soft organ music filtered out from the sanctuary. As I stood there holding my little dog, I felt like I was a part of some weird black and white Elia Kazan movie—one that when it was over, left the audience wondering what they'd seen.

Lined up behind me, an almost endless line of family and friends, their heads bowed in somber reverence. Jane's family had turned out in force. I had expected those from her father's side to be there, but her mom's side still surprised me. None of her mother's siblings were still alive, yet all but one of her cousins had made it to the funeral.

Before we went in, Powell, dressed in all his Methodist regalia, walked up to me and straightened my tie. As he did, he leaned over, placed his hand on Little Mutt's head and whispered in my ear, "God loves you and so does Little Mutt."

The service might have lasted an hour or just fifteen minutes. I had no way of tracking the time. My life had shifted into slow motion. I remember most of what took place, yet some things stood out more than others. I heard gasps as I walked in carrying Little Mutt in my arms. I tasted tears on my lips when we sang *Let There be Peace on Earth* and *Here I am Lord.* My nephew Walt read a poem, yet the only verse I remember was the last one, "I did not die." In his homily, Powell made reference to a statement many had made about Jane— "Someone once said, if there was such a thing as reincarnation, they'd want to come back as one of Jane Crayton's dogs." That brought snickers to the congregation.

And then there was Chantal. I first heard *Standing on Holy Ground* at the funeral of a very close friend. The song has always moved me. Later, I found out that the song had a similar effect on Barbara Streisand when she heard it at President Clinton's mother's funeral. Streisand was so moved by the song that she recorded it for her *Higher Ground* album.

Chantal is my favorite singer. Her voice has the classic purity of Beverly Sills coupled with the soulful rhythm of Etta James. Never before or since have I heard *Standing on Holy Ground* sung with the feeling and tone she sang it with that day. The gospel reverence that she put into that song, as if she sang for me only, stands out above anything else that I remembered about the service. And I know Jane approved.

Within what seemed like a cross between a couple of seconds and a few hours, we'd made our way from the church to the cemetery and back to my house. My house. Those words seem so strange. I'd never called it anything other than home or our house, but the words *"my house"* had such a hollow ring. The church had prepared lunch for the family and my close friends, but as the afternoon wore by, one by one they slowly disappeared. As the sun began to set, I found myself on the couch with Jimmy, Patti, and my cousin Fred. For the first time in more than three days, I began to peek under the tent at the loneliness that awaited me. The hurt had not gone away, it had only been bandaged and comforted by the throngs of loved ones who'd come to my aid. Now, for the first time in what had been a lifetime, I had to face life without Jane. A pain far beyond anything I'd ever imagined swept over me like an ocean wave, forcing me downward under its immense pressure, taking my breath from me in its effort to rip from me the very life that, with her, had been so precious. Part of me wanted to let go and allow the wave to send me into its life-ending riptide. But, for me, letting go had never been an option. I knew that no matter what I faced ahead of me, I had to continue up that long hill that had been my life. The obstacles had always been there. It had never been easy. But now, for the first time, I had to climb that hill in total darkness, *alone.*

Chapter
41

*B*Y FRIDAY, the fog I'd drifted in and out of slowly began to lift. Still, my life was a never-ending parade of confusion. Simple tasks gave way to unfinished ones. I'd no sooner start something, then walk away and do something else. I'd sit down to write thank you notes only to find myself sweeping the floor or gathering up laundry. Little things that I'd taken for granted seemed monumental. I'd never loaded a washing machine and felt too embarrassed to ask how the confounded thing worked. My life had turned into a series of jobs started and never completed. And everywhere I turned, I found memories of Jane—a song on the radio, a pair of shoes under the couch, her clothes hanging next to mine. The ones with tags still in them sent me into uncontrollable crying spells. And Little Mutt, my precious little girl, mourned in her own way, refusing to eat, moping around and spending much of her time lying on the floor looking like a mop with eyes—eyes that followed my every movement.

My grief had mushroomed into full depression. Reluctantly, I agreed to spend the weekend with Jimmy and Patti at their summerhouse. With Little Mutt in my lap in the back seat, the trip to eastern Carteret County passed quickly, and before I knew it, we were sitting on a swing underneath the huge live oaks that frame the quaint cottage. The thing that I remember most about that afternoon was the space that Jimmy and Patti gave me. I spent most of that afternoon sitting in the swing with my dog, pondering my surroundings and missing Jane terribly. With the loss of a loved one there are multitudes of firsts, each one brings back memories of time spent with that person. That afternoon, sitting in the swing at Jimmy's creek house was no exception. Visions of the times Jane and I had been there haunted me like a strange dream. Not just memories of the last time we'd been there, but a composite of all the times we'd spent there. By the time evening came, my brain was bursting with emotions. Then it happened.

As the sun began to set over the water, I felt a pull to be closer to it. Little Mutt and I walked to the end of the pier and found a place that left only the creek and the marsh beyond between us and the setting sun. Sunsets have been one of my favorite times of the day; especially those shared with Jane as we stood on the deck at our beach house and watched the winter sun slowly melt into the ocean. Holding on to one another, we'd gaze in quiet amazement at a spectacle we never tired of. And every time, just as the last ray of sunshine dipped below the water, Jane would always break the silence, sounding more like a little girl than a woman with the word "gone." As we sat there watching one of natures' grandest moments, I knew it would be the first sunset I'd see without her, but I knew I would never again hear her say the word "gone."

Most sunsets are ablaze in pinks, yellows, and oranges, and as this one began, it was no different. Then it all changed. The palate of colors slowly turned into blues, purples and golds. It was as if the sky had become the canvas of a watercolor painting. It was as if a painter was creating a celestial masterpiece. First, the sky became a wash of brilliant blues, darker at the top then lighter as the paint touched the now almost black marsh on the far shore. Then, as if by magic, clouds made their way to the canvas in hues of royal blue, soft purple and light grays. Just as one feature appeared, it would be followed by an even grander one. The reds and pinks of moments before had been transformed into brilliant golds as the painter methodically applied her brush to highlight the canvas.

When it was finished, the painting, framed only by the blackness of the marsh reflected in the creek and flowed across the water until it almost touched the edge of the dock where Little Mutt and I sat in startled amazement. It was as if we were not only just watching the sky unfold into the most beautiful painting I'd ever seen, we were a part of it.

Most sunset after-glows last fewer than twenty minutes before fading slowly into darkness. This one lasted for over an hour, never changing in composition, color or brilliance. When it was over, Little Mutt and I returned to Jimmy's porch.

"Could you believe that?" Patti asked.

At first I could not answer. My mind was still back in the moment. I pictured Jane looking down from Heaven at Little Mutt and me sitting on the end of the pier hurting beyond measure. It was as if she looked at God and said, "Please Master, do something. Skip hurts so badly. Let him know I'm okay and I'm here waiting for him."

"Jane, why don't you do it?" God answered.

"Me?" she asked. "How can I let him know?"

"My child, you are an artist. Paint him a sunset. He'll know it was from you."

When I finally spoke, I looked at my two best friends and wiped a tear from my cheek. "Jane just told me she was all right."

Life After Death

PART FOUR

"Son, one day you'll find a woman
who'll love you beyond all measure."

— *Paul Washington Crayton, Sr.*

169

Chapter 42

OR ALMOST FOUR YEARS, my main focus in life had been Jane. Everything else had been placed on hold, and I had no regrets.

In May of 2009, champion golfer Phil Mickelson found out that his wife had breast cancer. He immediately announced that his golf career would be put on hold indefinitely. A year and a half later, with his wife's disease in remission, he returned to golf. The following April as tears flowed down his cheeks, Mickelson hugged his precious wife when he won his third Master's title.

Contrast that to presidential candidate John Edwards who, when finding out that his wife Elizabeth's cancer had returned, decided to continue his ill-fated campaign. Could his commitment to his wife instead of the political campaign have helped him avoid his extra-marital affair and his eventual fall from grace? Would a decision to quit the race and attend to the needs of his wife have placed him in the position in eight years to be a major contender for the White House? That we'll never know, but it certainly shows the importance a single decision can have on our lives.

My commitment to Jane was never anything for me to question. I was bound and determined that she would get well. And now, knowing the outcome, I am more than thankful that I was with her until the end. Not one day in those years did I ever regret that commitment. Instead, I thanked God every day for the opportunity to be a part of her life. And when it ended, the memory of her squeezing my hand as she took her last breath will live within me until I take my last.

Now for the first time in almost forty years, I had no one to look after but myself, or at least me and Little Mutt. Of course, that was something for which I had never planned. I had always expected to die before Jane.

To say that the sadness had ended or even subsided a little would be a gross overstatement. It now lived in a special corner of my mind—occasionally coming out, sometimes like a kitten and other times like a lion— almost never when I was prepared.

Before Jane died, she'd told me that she wanted me to continue on, even to get married again. Usually, I swept those conversations under the rug and changed the subject. Sometimes I almost felt as if there was someone she'd even picked out for me.

It had now been more than four months since Jane had died and yet strangely enough, I'd never felt lonely. I don't know whether it was some sort of relief that came from the pressure we'd endured during the last three and a half years or just some sort of newfound freedom that I was experiencing. Having no one else to look after was a completely new experience. Either way, each carried with it a bit of guilt.

And the guilt increased as I found myself thinking about sex again. It had been several years since Jane and I had been sexually intimate, and the thought of a new experience both excited me and shamed me all at the same time. I guess the excitement had to do with something new and long overdue, coupled with the shame that I'd be cheating on Jane, made for confusion for which I'd never prepared myself. But never the less, as much as I tried to suppress the thoughts, they crept to the forefront of my thinking like a thirsty man told not to think about water. Was I obsessed? No. But still, the thoughts would not go away.

I guess much of that kind of thinking may have been fueled by what other men who'd been in similar situations called "the casserole queens." Well-intentioned friends and acquaintances slowly began to mention the names of single women friends close to my age. Some of those female friends had been urged, out of the kindness of their hearts and without an intentional motive, to make sure that I did not starve to death. By the time Thanksgiving rolled around, both my upright freezers were full of frozen casseroles. I never looked at such kindness as anything more than intended and I am forever thankful for every dish and thought. It didn't take long for the well-intended to realize that I was not ready for a relationship, and if one did occur, it would be of my own making.

Fortunately I didn't have to go completely without female companionship. Over the years I'd had the opportunity to build close friendships with some very interesting and successful women. One such person is my friend Nancy Stallings.

Nancy had been a good friend of both Jane and me. It was at her house that the supper club had been held the weekend that Jane got so sick. As the director of the NC Global Transpark Foundation, a job perfectly suited for her charismatic ability to balance politicians and business leaders, she had been one of the few single women Jane respected. There was never a hint of competition between them. From the first day Jane got sick until she died, Nancy was a part of our inner circle; a person we both loved and trusted.

Many a time during beach weekends Jane would go to bed early and leave Nancy and me up as we'd discuss politics into the wee hours of the morning—Nancy taking the Democratic Party line with me always being the devil's advocate. Asking the next morning if we'd solved the problems of the world, Nancy's answer would always be the same. "Jane, he is so impossible. I don't know how you can live with that man."

Just as she'd been there for me and Jane, Nancy helped me through one of the toughest times of my life. We'd never been attracted to one another, but we had a strong friendship and deep mutual respect. I needed a woman I could have over for dinner or take out for a drink after work—someone I could just sit with and watch television. And someone I could talk with. I had so many questions, especially about being single at my age, about relationships, and about sex.

As usual, Nancy was always straight with me and did not just tell me what I wanted to hear but gave me good direction. And when the women did start to surface in my life, women like the "biker chic," the "very" young younger woman, and the office worker from a past life, none of whom I wanted to start a relationship with, it was Nancy and her guidance that helped me stay on track.

Chapter 43

FROM THE TIME Jane got sick in 2001 until she died, I'd barely left her side. My whole life had been focused on finding a liver or a miracle. As time passed and her name dropped further down the list, I felt that—on occasion—I could be away from her for a night or two. The first time happened when I went with my brother to hook up with his son Walt to go to a Carolina basketball game. The other time was a two-day trip to the Tire Bowl in Charlotte.

After Jane died, I reluctantly agreed to take a trip to the UNC-Miami football game with my brother, my nephew, and several other guys. Again, God picked me up and sent me where he wanted to be. I had not been on an airplane since 9/11. I had not been on a trip of any length in more than six years, and suddenly here I was with a new world unfolding around me. I'd never checked in at an airport for just one person. I'd never walked through an airport without two or three carry-ons wrapped across my shoulders. Everything in my life had been based on two. Now it was one.

Those four days in Miami were incredible. For the first time in what seemed a lifetime, I was having a good time. And I didn't feel guilty. I felt like Jane was smiling down from heaven. At fifty-nine, I felt brand new again. That weekend, there were many firsts: first time I'd been to the Orange Bowl, first time I'd had dinner at

Emeril Lagossi's and the first time I'd paid twenty dollars for a bourbon and water. But I'd also been to Collins Avenue in South Beach, eaten at great restaurants, been to football games, had drinks at the Fontainebleau Hotel, and walked the streets of South Miami Beach. Yet it was as if it was all new to me. Each experience felt like a first.

Oh, and there was one more first. In 1997, the famous international designer Giovanni Versace was killed in Miami Beach. The story made the national press along with the tabloids. At the center of his murder was his Venetian "style" mansion located on Ocean Boulevard in the middle of trendy South Miami Beach. Since Versace's death, the house eventually passed into the hands of Peter Loftin, a New Bern native and the founder of BTI Telecommunications Company. The entire time we were in Miami, all the news shows were reporting the upcoming Halloween Party being hosted at the mansion. After dinner that night, we decided to go over to the mansion and watch the guests arriving. As we approached, we saw TV satellite trucks, searchlights and an endless line of limousines filled with the rich and famous. As each group arrived, a TV talking head stopped the celeb's for a short interview much in an Academy-Awards-type ceremony.

As we stood across the street watching, I noticed that the costumes these folks were wearing did not come from Wal-Mart. Most looked as if they came from central casting at some Hollywood studio—Batman looked like Batman, Marilyn Monroe looked like Marilyn.

Just as we were about to leave, one of the guys in the group, Mike O'Daniel, said, "Hey, I think I see Pete. Come on, guys. Let's go to the party."

As Mike started across the street, followed by the rest of us like his entourage, I grabbed his son, Parker. "Is your dad crazy?"

"He and Pete Loftin grew up together. They were best friends." Parker laughed.

Moments later, we were all standing in the main hall of the Versace mansion, with "run of the house" wrist bands, staring at some of the most beautiful women I'd ever seen in my life. The trip to Miami allowed me to escape from my reality and to peep around the corner into the land of the living.

I WAS UPBEAT AND HAPPY as I opened the back door and walked into my house. It had been fifteen years since I'd been up that late. But two in the morning in South Beach was not considered that late. Before I could set my bag down, Little Mutt charged around the corner, leapt into my arms, and washed my face with her tongue. As I stood there holding her, I could tell that something was different and not just with me. Little Mutt was different as well. She'd stopped moping around. She was full of life again.

It was as if she was saying to me, "Okay, Dad. It's time for us both to get back to the land of the living."

Chapter
44

*A*S THE HOLIDAY season approached, I found myself wondering how it would be different this year. Thanksgiving had always been one of my favorite holidays. But for Jane, it was a day to endure and get through as painlessly as possible. Her sister, Ann, died on Thanksgiving Day. Twelve years later, her father died on Thanksgiving Day. In 2003, three days before Thanksgiving, her mother passed away. So it was no wonder that Thanksgiving held so many painful memories for her. It was a day Jane had to get through as quickly as possible. For as much as I loved Thanksgiving, it became a solemn day spent with Jane's parents, then with her mother, and finally with just the two of us.

For Jane, Christmas started the day after Thanksgiving. For me, the only rule I'd laid down was that decorating for Christmas could not start until the day after Thanksgiving, allowing me some degree of reverence for that special day.

My first Thanksgiving without Jane would be different. I planned to spend the day with my family. My favorite Thanksgiving song as a child was "Over the River and Through the Woods, to Grandmother's House We Go." With only one grandparent nearby for the kids, it was traditional for my family to gather at my brother's house. That year, my sister-in-law had heard

178

of a program where locals would share the day with young Marine's from the nearby base at Cherry Point who couldn't make it home for Thanksgiving. Instead of being a difficult day for me, that Thanksgiving soared all the way to the top of my list of holidays, where it now stays.

We shared our meal and fellowship with three Marine privates—a girl from Pennsylvania, a guy from Florida, and one from California. All were just eighteen years old, and it was their first Thanksgiving away from their families. To say that we received more than we gave by having those kids with us is a huge understatement. With all the emotions of that first time without Jane, I honestly can say that my heart was soothed and comforted by the presence of those three young Marines.

Finally, I'd had a Thanksgiving like the ones I'd remembered as a kid and that day, as I thanked God for all my many blessings, I thanked Him for that special day.

Now I could look toward Christmas, but again I'd made up my mind that this year would be different. I knew that Jane would not be with me, and I knew that I would miss her terribly; that the emotions of the season would surely have a magnified effect on me. But I had made up my mind that for the first time in my adult life, my approach to the season would be different. Instead of charging into the preparations head-on, that year I wanted the Christmas season to slowly unfold in front of me like a sunrise—first starting as a glow in the eastern sky, then breaking the horizon as a small orange ball, only to finally light the day with its golden brilliance. I wanted to be a part of every moment.

To say that Jane Crayton was a high maintenance woman would be like saying that a car needs a daily oil change. This wasn't just as she became sick, Jane had always been that way and I didn't mind. I knew how

179

she was before I ever married her. There were certain things that she simply would not do, like taking the garbage to the street. Many a time, she'd call my office when I'd forgotten to get the can to the curb to remind me that it was garbage day. Dutifully, I'd jump in my car, drive to the house, and take the can to the street. Even the few times the thought occurred to me to ask Jane to do it, I knew that would never happen. One day in jest, I told her that if I ever wanted to hide a present from her, all I had to do was to place it next to the garage can and she'd never find it.

And Christmas was the time she required the most maintenance. I didn't just have to change the oil daily, I had to rotate the tires, and wash and wax the metaphorical car. She was Santa Clause, and I was her elf. Jane made the plans, and I hung the wreaths. She picked out the "live" trees and I put them in the stands, carried them in the house and hung the lights, which, by the way, never seemed to work the next year. Jane bought the presents and I wrapped them—what seemed like hundreds of presents. One year, to expedite my wrapping chores, I bought a commercial-sized roll of red paper and one of those roll cutters like department stores use.

The never-ending list of things to do began the day after Thanksgiving and stopped on Christmas night. To say that I am one of those who have what some call the Christmas "depression" would be a mistake, because most of the time I enjoyed the season. It was such a special time for Jane. But once in a while, I'd complain about how the workload got in the way of experiencing the season: things like driving down Spencer Avenue—the most decorated street in town—and marveling at the lights, dropping in on friends unexpectedly, or having time to ponder that just-right gift for a special friend.

One year, before Jane got sick, I really got fed up. I felt as if everyone had lost the real meaning of Christmas. I decided to put my feelings on paper. The piece called "Where is Christmas?" began with my anger toward what I believed Christmas had become and ended with the hope found in those who saw the true spirit of Christmas. I felt so good about what I'd written; I sent it to our local newspaper. On Christmas Eve, it appeared on the editorial page right next to a reprint of the famous *New York Sun Editorial,* "Yes Virginia, There is a Santa Clause."

Chapter
45

*F*OR THE FIRST TIME IN MY LIFE, the holiday season was going to be different. Christmas day this year would be the destination. Like crossing the Atlantic on the QE2, I planned to enjoy the journey. Sure, I knew there would be emotional pitfalls, but I needed to experience them, as well. Joy does not always mean happiness. It is a part of us, if we let it live in us. And sometimes we can experience joy and sadness all at the same time. The first time I heard Faith Hill's *Where are You Christmas*, I had to pull into a parking lot and stop for a moment. My tears flowed so heavily that I could not see. At the beginning of the song, Hill laments the pain of loss that clouds her vision of Christmas, but as the song ends, it does so with hope and confirmation that there will be a Christmas in her life.

I decided that I wanted to decorate the house, not with the vigor that Jane had done, but I did want my home to look like Christmas. I even picked out a live tree. One night with the help of Larry and Annie and Jimmy and Patti, we put together a close facsimile of what the house had looked like when Jane was alive. When they all left, I sat down on the couch with Little Mutt in my lap and smiled. It felt good to see things looking like Christmas. That's when the phone rang.

"How's the house look?" my brother asked.

"Frank, it's really beginning to feel like Christmas," I said. "I'm going to take part in it all."

"Good," Frank continued. "That's why I called. When was the last time you went to the Realtor-Home Builder Christmas Ball?"

Sitting back, I pulled my hand through my hair. "Damn, I don't know. Fifteen, twenty years, I guess."

The Ball used to be the biggest, most well-attended Christmas party in town. In years gone by, it was considered to be the best party of the season.

"Well, Skip, this year you're going to go with us." Frank caught me off-guard. Experiencing an old remembered Christmas was one thing, but going to a party was another.

"I don't know," I said, searching for any excuse. "I'm sure I'd never be able to fit into my tuxedo."

"No problem," Frank had already loaded both barrels and blasted away. "Penneys has them on sale for $125.00 including the shirt, tie, and studs."

I held the phone and thought. *Why not? I won't have to stay out late and I'll know everyone there, so I won't feel like a fifth wheel.* "Okay. I'll go."

"Great," Frank said. I could almost hear him smiling. "Dana and I will pick you up around 6:30."

"That sounds fine. By the way, when is it?"

"Oh yeah that might be a good idea. It's Friday night, December 10—less than two weeks away. You better get over to Penneys."

I flipped my phone closed and stuck it back in my pocket. I wondered if I was ready to go to a party. I wanted to walk again among the living, but would this be a little too soon? Not once, however, did I wonder what others might say. Years before, I'd adopted a slogan that drove my father crazy. *What you think of me is none of my business.* To continue living was my decision, I was not going to bounce the idea off anyone else.

The days of the "Old South" ended when Rhett Butler shocked a fund-raising event in Atlanta when he asked a still mourning Scarlett O'Hara to dance. As they whirled around the dance floor with Scarlet dressed in her black *widow's weeds*, her aunt Pity Pat fainted. The days of a mandatory twelve-month grieving period, like the years before the Civil War, were *Gone with the Wind*, or at least that's what I thought. Unfortunately, there are some things that die very slowly in the South.

Chapter
46

GOD PLACES US exactly where he wants us to be. We may call it chance, but for Him there is no chance. A week before the ball, God placed me in the copy room at my office. As I stood in front of the machine feeding papers into the copier, I overheard two agents talking. One said that she had just had lunch with Carol Dail and that the subject of the Christmas Ball had come up. Hearing Carol's name and the ball come up at the same time perked my interest. Without turning, I continued to eavesdrop.

"She's going, isn't she?" the agent asked.

"I don't know. One of her best customers has asked her to be their guest and sit at their table. Otherwise, she told me that there is no way she'd go to the ball by herself. It's just that Carol doesn't feel that she can turn them down."

I slowed my paper feeding down and listened as the other agent continued. "That's right. I forgot, she's single. That could be a little awkward."

"I don't think the Ball is the worst part for her. She told me that if she could just find someone to walk in the front door with, she could handle the rest." The agent fished some papers from her "in-box" and turned toward the door.

"Maybe she'll find someone," the agent replied. "At least if she goes, she can go out and buy a new dress."

185

I heard a chuckle from the hallway. "There's always an upside."

I grabbed my copies, returned to my office; leaned back in my chair and propped my feet up on the desk wondering what had just happened. Hearing Carol's name jolted me like a loud clap of thunder. My mind drifted back to the first time I met her.

The Home Builders' Golf Tournament is a huge event here in New Bern. Teams are selected to play a super ball or captain's choice, where each person takes a shot after which the best shot is picked and it repeats itself for eighteen holes. The format is a lot of fun as it allows bad golfers to participate and also produces some really low scores. For the previous two years, I'd played on a team sponsored by one of the mortgage companies.

The third year, one of the guys couldn't make the event so we ended up with a new player on our team. Boy, was I surprised when a girl walked up and placed her golf bag in the cart. Not only was she a woman, she was a nice-looking woman and the only woman in the tournament. As we began to play, I found out that she was one thing else: one hell of a golfer. We designated one of the guys our "A" or best player. Another the "B" player, Carol was to be the "C" golfer and I took up the rear. That day Carol could have been anybody's "A" player. When the tournament was over, we'd won second place.

There was something about Carol that drew me to her. It was not sexual nor was it anything I could really put my finger on. Jane was in the first year of her disease, and I was wholly committed to her and very much in love. It wasn't that I was attracted to Carol. There was just something about her that I liked.

For the next year, our paths crossed occasionally, but only professionally. I respected her as an appraiser. She not only did her work on time, she knew what she was doing, and unlike a lot of appraisers that I knew, she worked on Saturdays if she needed to get the work out. When she asked me to sign her copy of *Remember When* I made it out "To Carol, my favorite appraiser."

The following year at the Home Builders' tournament, the same team played again and this time Carol and I rode together. Still, I knew very little about her. I'd found out that we'd shared the same piano teacher, that she had a young son, Sam, and that she had grown up in the Spring Garden area. I also knew that Carol was not married. I assumed she was divorced.

That was the sum total of everything I knew about Carol Dail as I sat in my office wondering why the thought of being her *Knight in Shining Armor* and walking her into the Convention Center had ever entered my mind. Almost ashamed by my thoughts, I quickly tried to shove them away. But as much as I tried, my thoughts of Carol would not go way. Three days later, I picked up the phone and called her.

Chapter
47

I THINK I dialed her number three times before I pushed the send button on my cell phone. I'd told myself over and over that this was not going to be a date; I was only helping a friend. When she answered, I told her that I'd heard that she was going to be at the ball.

Carol made it easy. "I guess so," she said. "The only thing is that I hate to walk in there by myself."

Carol opened the door and I slowly slid my foot in it.

"That's, uh, part of why I called," I stuttered. "I overheard a couple of girls at the office talking the other day and that's what I thought they'd said. Look, I'm going with my brother and his wife, and if you'd like, you can ride with us so you won't have to go in by yourself."

The dead silence at her end made me look down at my phone to make sure it hadn't dropped the call. Finally she answered. "Are you sure?"

"Yeah, it won't really be a date or anything." My heart skipped a couple of beats and my hand trembled. "We'll just ride together and I'll walk in with you. Then you can sit with your crowd and I'll sit with my crowd."

"Are you sure?" she asked again.

"Yeah, I'm sure. We could meet at my house around six and have a glass of wine before my brother picks us up."

"Is your brother okay with this?" she asked.

"Of course. When I told them about the conversation I'd overheard, they thought this would be a great idea."

"Skip, this is such a relief," she said. "I can't thank you enough. I've fretted over this thing for more than a week. You just don't know how much I appreciate this."

"Well great." Relief washed over me like a cool breeze on a summer day. "Then okay, it's a date... er... I mean it's not really a date, it's a..."

Carol interrupted. "Skip, I know what you mean. I'll see you at six on Friday."

As I hung up my phone, I felt the blood slowly scroll across my face, its warm rush replacing the coolness of the breeze that had just washed over me.

I cannot remember the actual date that I'd called Carol or much else that took place between that call and December 10. But I do remember the day of the ball. I'd said to myself over and over that going with Carol to the ball was not a date, just a gentlemanly gesture—a Lancelot and Guinevere thing.

"Then why are you so nervous," I asked myself. I felt like I did the first time I went to the prom when I was a junior in high school. I think I started preparing for our non-date that morning. I went to the grocery store and picked up some boiled shrimp and dip and crackers of some kind. As I strolled by the flower department, I felt an urge to pick up something. I've mentioned my "little voice" before, but sometimes there are two that live inside me. And from time to time they battle each other. This day, they fought one another like junkyard dogs.

One said, "Go on Skip, get her a dozen roses." Then the other countered, "Give me a break, man, it's not even a date. What are you going to do when you really ask someone out? Give 'em a diamond?"

"Why don't you both shut up," I said. "Let me do this my way." I won the argument, so I bought her a single long-stemmed red rose.

Before I went upstairs to shower and change, I fussed about the kitchen chilling the wine and picking the "just right" dish for the snacks. Just as I finished, the phone rang.

"Are you getting excited?" Jimmy asked.

"It's really not a date," I tried to convince my best friend, but he knew me all too well.

"Oh yeah, that's right," his sarcasm hissed through the phone. "I forgot. It's a 'giving a girl a ride to the convention center and walking her to her table' kind of thing. And I guess you told her to meet you in your driveway so the two of you can wait for Frank to pick you up."

"Jimmy," I scolded. "She's going to stop by and have a glass of wine before Frank comes. I even have some shrimp and cocktail sauce as an hors d'oeuvre."

"Hmmmm." I could almost see his expression over the phone, a look I'd seen many times before. "And flowers, you know women love flowers. But wait, this is not really a date. You'd only give her flowers if it was a real date."

For a moment I'd wondered if Jimmy had heard the battle of the voices. "Well, yes. I did."

"Flowers?"

"Not flowers," I drug out the s. "Flower."

"A single long-stemmed red rose, I'll bet. You romantic dog, you."

"Yes," I whispered.

I didn't need an amplifier to hear what was going on at the other end. "Patti, he's got shrimp and wine for his non-date, but you won't believe the rest...a single long-stemmed red rose."

"That's my boy," I heard Patti say in the background.

I looked at my watch. "Jimmy, I gotta go get dressed. I'll call you in the morning and tell you all about it."

"I can't wait. But, listen, when you tell me, start off with one of your stupid similes like *I could have danced all night,* if you have a good time."

"You got it. I've really got to go."

"Talk to you in the morning."

"Bye," I said as I hung up and started upstairs.

Chapter 48

I THINK I got downstairs a little before six. Putting on a tux has never been a chore for me. My father gave me my first one as a high school graduation present, figuring I'd need one when I was off at college. He was right.

Time crawled like ketchup from a bottle. My watch refused to move. I must have looked at it twenty times as I set out the shrimp and carefully placed the rose on the table between the couches. Finally as all the hands pointed down, I noticed a flash of headlights reflect across the living room windows. *I'll bet that's her,* I thought. Minutes later I checked my watch again. *It doesn't take that long to walk from a car to the front porch,* I thought. Then I heard the knock on the front door followed by Little Mutt's bark as she ran into the foyer.

Three giant steps later, I stood at the door, or maybe I just flew there, I don't remember.

I'd told Carol where I lived and that my front doors were painted pink. I found out later why it took so long for her to knock. As she stood on the porch Carol pushed the doorbell button once, twice, then finally a third time. Afraid she'd come to the wrong house almost caused her to turn away. Finally she knocked. I'd forgotten to tell her that my doorbell didn't work.

Carol and I had known each other for just over a year and a half. Other than our time playing together in the golf tournament, I'd probably never been in her company more than three or four other times for a total of maybe two hours. I'd only seen her in shorts or jeans. I'd never seen her dressed up.

No one has ever called me "speechless," but when I opened the door, I was dumbfounded. Carol stepped into the foyer wearing a long black gown and a short sequined jacket. Her reddish brown hair glinted with highlights and her makeup looked natural and exciting. Talk about being blown over by a feather. She looked ravishing. I think I fell in love with her right then and there.

When I helped her with her jacket, I got to the rest of the prize. The dress revealed her arms and shoulders. And I began to melt. "Wow, you've got beautiful shoulders," was all that came out of my mouth.

"And who are you?" Carol asked, reaching down to pet Little Mutt.

"Carol, meet Little Mutt, the one girl in my life."

Carol rubbed her head and Little Mutt responded her approval by wagging her tail. "You must smell Socker. He's my little dog."

I led Carol into the family room. She took a seat on one couch and I sat down on the one opposite her. Before I offered her a glass of wine, I presented her with the rose. Carol took it, smelled the flower and nodded her approval as Little Mutt jumped up on the couch and snuggled next to her.

"You've won her over," I said.

That part of the evening was a blur to me. I was so mesmerized that I remember little of what we talked about other than she told me that the next day, she and her son Sam would be leaving at 5:30 a.m. to go to Pascagoula, Mississippi, on a church mission trip to repair roofs damaged by Hurricane Katrina.

Our time together flew by so quickly that well before we finished our wine, I heard Frank open the back door and announce that our coach had arrived. My modern-day Cinderella story had already started to unfold.

The ride to the convention center was filled with small talk. When Dana asked her about her son, Carol proudly told her that Sam would be going to college at Campbell University the next fall on an academic scholarship, something that both excited and worried her all at the same time. It would be the first time that Sam had left the nest, and as a parent she was concerned about him being away but happy for his opportunity. For Carol, it would be the first time in eighteen years that she'd be alone without him. As Carol and Dana talked, I could not keep my eyes off of her.

Frank parked the car in front of the convention center and the four of us walked to the building. "Take my arm," I said to Carol as we walked to the front door. "It's time for me to get on my white horse and do my thing."

Proudly, I walked my *non-date* into the building and into the ballroom. As I looked around, I knew that I had the prettiest girl in the room. I beamed. What began as an offer to rescue a damsel in distress became a moment of extreme pleasure for me. I was living a dream. As we walked past my brother's table where I was supposed to sit, I turned to him and said, "Frank, if I can find a seat at Carol's table. I'm sitting with her tonight."

Sure enough when we got to her table, there was an empty seat. And the magic didn't stop there. We danced and talked and shared our dreams that night. The chemistry between the two of us seemed to ignite the room. More energy than chemistry, it was as if we glowed. It felt as though a spotlight was on us the entire evening. We basked with the attention. People we

194

both knew spoke and nodded their approval. Everyone there seemed to be pulling for us to get together.

When the evening was over, Frank and Dana dropped us off at my house. Carol and I went in for a cup of coffee. When it came time for her to leave, I walked her to her car and asked if I could see her again.

"I'd like that very much," Carol said as she unlocked her car. "But with all you've been through, let's just take it slow and easy."

"Sure," I answered. "Slow and easy. That works for me, but can I call you next week?"

"Remember, I'll be in Mississippi and might not get the call. But you can leave me a message and I'll call you back."

Before she got in her car, we hugged each other. As Carol drove away, I stood in my driveway watching until her taillights disappeared down the street. My Cinderella night had come to an end, but unlike that fairy tale, my Cinderella didn't dash off at the stroke of midnight, leaving her glass slipper behind. My fairy tale had just begun. I was left with the hope of seeing her again.

I don't think I got to sleep before three. It had been a lifetime since I'd felt like I did that night. I'd had the time of my life, and I did not want the feeling to end.

Chapter
49

$\mathcal{S}$ATURDAY MORNING CAME EARLY. New Bern High School, my alma mater, was playing in the State 4-A football championship game that afternoon in Raleigh and I had a book signing at Borders in Cary that morning. Debby was going to be picking me up by 10:00 a.m. I started the coffee maker and called Jimmy.

"Okay," he said when he answered the phone. "Was it *My Fair Lady?*"

"No," I replied. "It was more like *Dirty Dancing.*"

For a moment the phone went dead. "I'm so sorry," Jimmy said.

His demeanor quickly changed when I broke into my rendition of Jennifer Warnes' song, *I Had the Time of My Life.*

"Tell me every detail so I can share them with Patti."

His excitement and joy for me came through the phone like a Sousa march. I could almost hear the brass band tuning up. Euphoria swept over me along with an emptiness in my gut. I wanted to see her again. I missed her.

"Why do I have these feelings?" I asked myself. "I'm mourning the loss of my wife, but the feelings are there; feelings for another person, another woman."

Guilt crept over me like rain clouds over a full moon on a dark stormy night—a storm with no lightning, just the gloom of thunder and clouds. *I can't let this overwhelm me,* I thought. *Last night was real. It was wonderful. I didn't do anything wrong.*

The battle inside me continued throughout the day. Fortunately, the book signing and the football game distracted me for a while.

Yet on the drive back, as my niece and her friends slept in the back seat of my sister's Tahoe, my mind slowly drifted back to Carol. I knew there was something special about her, that we had not connected simply by chance. The magic of the night before was not magic at all. This was real, a gift from God. Slowly I began to win the battle with my dark side. That night, the thunder and clouds that had plagued my thinking, rolled back, revealing the light of a freshly dawning day. I knew my life was about to change.

God speaks to us every day, but unfortunately we miss his signs. I believe that miracles come in all sizes—some as dramatic as an airplane landing safely on the Hudson River to a doctor removing a wart. Some miracles prevent an immediate catastrophe and some a long-term one. God's messages come in all forms. A word from a friend, a thought, and even a song. For most of my life, God has been sending me messages. The only problem has been that I've missed many of them. Either I'd not been paying attention or listening. A part of me was beginning to wake up. For the first time in my life, I started to pay attention.

For me on that drive home, it came in the form of a song by Andy Griggs, *If Heaven*[2]. As I listened to the song, for the first time the words jumped out of the speaker as if the song had been written with me in mind. It was like Jane knew what my heart was feeling and asked God to speak to me through Andy's song.

---

[2] *If Heaven*, written by Gretchen Peters. Released by Andy Greggs 2004

*If heaven were a town, it would be
my town on a summer day in 1965,*
    *And everything I wanted was out
there and everyone I loved was still
alive,*
    *If Heaven was a tear, it would be my
last one and you'd be in my arms again,*
    *Don't cry a tear for me now, baby,
there comes a time when we all must
say goodbye. And if that's what
heaven's made of, you know, I ain't
afraid to die.*

"You all right?" Debby asked, noticing the tears streaming down my face.

"Who was that?" I asked, referring to the song.

"Andy Griggs." My sister reached over and patted me on the leg. "It's a real good song."

"It touched my heart."

Debby pursed her lips and nodded. "I know."

Chapter
50

*P*RINCE CHARMING had a glass slipper. All I had was a phone number, and I struggled with the thought of calling Carol. The nagging in my head started again. One voice told me to call and the other reminded me what she'd said about taking things slowly. It had been more than forty years since I'd thought about dating or how to approach a woman. My life had been pretty well set. Now all of a sudden, I didn't know what to do.

At times, I tend to wear my emotions on my sleeve. It certainly didn't take the girls at the office long to figure out what was going on. I must have been moping around like some sort of lovesick puppy. One day one of the agents in the office, Martha Cook, asked. "Have you called her?"

Martha Cook is a blonde with a model's figure, the brains of a CEO, and a personality that makes her the perfect real estate agent: both husband and wife when working with her feel comfortable in her presence. She reminds me of how I'd have loved for my daughter Mary Ruth to have turned out. I once told her father that if my daughter had lived, I'd have wanted her to be just like Martha. I trust her. Martha has "street smarts." It hadn't been that long since she'd been in the dating scene.

"No, I haven't," I said, looking down at my shoes.

"Why not?" she asked.

"I don't know. Carol said she wanted us to take things slow." I leaned against the wall and looked up toward the ceiling.

"Call her," Martha spread her feet apart and placed her hands on her hips. "I guarantee you she'll be happy to hear from you."

"You sure?" I shook my head.

"I saw how y'all looked at each other Friday night. There was something magical between the two of you."

"There's that word again. All magic is nothing but make believe."

"Call it what you want. What I saw was real. Call her."

I walked over and gave her a hug. "That's exactly what I needed to hear."

Before I made the call, I must have practiced what I planned to say at least a dozen times. When I finally mustered up enough nerve to call, I got her voicemail.

Two days later as I was driving home for lunch, my cell phone rang and her number popped up. My heart pounded so hard, I ran off the road trying to answer the call. I don't remember anything about the conversation. Everything I'd practiced flew out the window. I think I asked how the work was going and how her son was doing. I do remember asking if I could call back and she told me it would be all right. When we hung up, I thanked God, and then realized I'd never met Sam.

Two days later, I had been out walking Little Mutt when I decided to call her again. Expecting voicemail, I was actually surprised when she answered. Again, small talk dominated the call, but before she hung up, I asked her when she would be back. When she said Saturday, I took a deep breath and asked her if I could go with her to church on Sunday.

If I'd been standing on the top of the Empire State, Building what I heard next would have sent my heart plummeting eighty-six stories. "Skip, we need to move

200

slowly. I'm afraid for us to do something like going to church together would be too soon. Anyway, I've got a meeting about the mission trip right after church."

Without thinking I shot back, "Carol I haven't done anything like this in over forty years. I don't understand this thing about going slow. All I know is that I want to see you again. I want to get to know you. I'd like to see if that thing that happened between us last Friday night was real. I felt it and I think you did, too."

"Yes," she said. "I felt it, too. But I—right now, I'm really confused. Something's going on inside me that I haven't felt in a long time. I need some time to think." Through her words, I could almost hear her heart beating.

"Fair enough," I said. "You take all the time you need. Call me when you're ready."

"I'll call you when I get back."

"Be careful. I'll talk to you then. Goodbye."

"Goodbye."

I flipped my phone shut and reached into the basement of my soul, picked up my heart, and tried to tell it that everything was going to be all right. But with all the pain it had suffered, all I heard was a strong "I told you so" from one of my voices telling me that I'd probably never hear from Carol again. One thing, however, kept me from feeling like a fool. My other voice whispered, "It's not over. Remember whatever it was that you'd felt, she said she felt it, too."

Chapter
51

$\mathcal{S}$OMETIMES all we need is a small ray of hope to hang onto, and the rest of the week I clung tightly to the hope that one day soon I would hear from Carol. I never thought it would be as soon as Saturday. I was in the backyard when the phone rang, but I can't recall what I was doing. One thing I can recall was that I didn't pick up the phone, electing to let the call go into voicemail. That feather popped me beside the head again when I later saw Carol's number. I didn't pause a second before I called her back.

When Carol answered, I heard the glow in her voice and my heart quickened. As we talked, she apologized about church and explained that she had a meeting and the time would not be good. Then she opened the door for our first date. "I would like to see you next week, if you'd like to."

"How about lunch?" I asked.

"I'd like that very much," she said.

"How's Tuesday?" My eyes lit up and a grin swept across my face. "Capt'n Ratty's?"

"Works for me."

"Then it's a date," I said.

"A real date?" she asked.

"You bet. I'll see you at noon."

When we hung up I picked up Little Mutt and we danced across the deck.

MY BROTHER will be late for his own funeral. Time, for him, is something that other people worry about. Being late doesn't bother him at all. But for me, I've always felt like being punctual is a way of telling the people you are about to meet that they matter. When I got to the restaurant a few minutes early, Carol was already there.

As I took my seat at the corner table, I reached over and touched her hand. Carol glanced up at me with warm, caring eyes. I immediately felt relaxed and comfortable. At first, the conversation tended more toward small talk, but the door cracked open when I asked her about the Mississippi trip. She lit up like a flash of lightning dancing across the sky and I quickly found out that she had a real "heart for missions." I listened as she shared the story, how she'd even run across some old friends from a different time in her life, all with the same goal of helping others. What touched me most was what she said had been the highlight of the trip. "You know Skip, we all went down to help. But when I left that place, deep in my heart I felt I'd received far more than I'd given." From that point on, the door between us swung wide open and what unfolded in front of us for the next three hours was not just the history of our lives, but our stories.

I learned about Carol's three brothers and her parents, how she grew up on a farm, loved sports, about the time she got hit in the mouth with a baseball bat and her embarrassment at having her front teeth fixed. She told me how, with the help of her mom and dad, she'd worked her way through Atlantic Christian College where she'd played on the women's basketball team.

As she continued telling me her story, she reminded me that we'd even shared the same piano teacher,

203

albeit, at different times in our lives. I couldn't believe that our paths had never crossed. She and her family had lived during my lifetime on Spring Garden Road, less than ten miles from town, and I knew nothing about them. I would eventually find out that I'd tried to sell her brother Robert and his wife Naomi a house back in 1969, but I would not connect those dots until a year or so later.

"I can't believe I never met your oldest brother, Junior," I broke in. "We're the same age, how come we never knew each other?"

A sly smile crossed her face. "Didn't you say you knew my cousin Jimmy?"

I shook my head. "Yeah, that's what I mean. Jimmy Dail was in my class. How come I didn't know at least one of your brothers? Did y'all go to some private school?"

Carol's eyes sparkled and the sly smile turned into a grin. She answered me with a question. "When you were at New Bern High, how many high schools were there in Craven County?"

Without thinking I quickly answered, "Two. New Bern and Havelock."

"What about Vanceboro?" she asked, the grin getting larger.

Without realizing I was being set up, I replied, "Oh yeah, Farm Life High School. I forgot about them. Rough place to play basketball. Those guys slashed the tires on our bus one time when we beat them. Y'all went to Farm Life?"

"No." Her smiled erupted into a laugh. "There were two more high schools in Craven County then: Dover and Jasper. We all went to Jasper High School."

"You're kidding me?"

She reached over and touched my hand and shook her head. "Oh, how insulated you city boys were."

Chapter 52

"*N*OW TELL ME all about Sam," I said. For a moment she got quiet, almost distant—her eyes moist as she gazed at the ceiling. She looked back at me as if there was something else she wanted to say. When the hesitation ended, she regained composure as she began telling me all about her son. With each word, I could see her demeanor change as she moved from that moment of pause to the excitement of sharing Sam with me. I knew right then that he was the most important person in the world to Carol, and I not only loved hearing every word she had to say about him, but watching how she said them.

I learned that Sam was on the golf team at school that he loved to fish, but didn't get to go as much as he'd like, that he was an honor roll student, had brown hair and stood six-foot-two. I also found out that he had been dating a girl who went to New Bern High for more than a year and that her name was Jane. I knew that Carol was a single parent, but I'd just guessed she was divorced. She told me that she'd never been married. She had decided not to marry Sam's birth father. When I asked if the two of them saw one another, she told me that they did, but she was the parent who had raised Sam. I decided to leave that subject for another time. Then she told me about the drive back from Mississippi.

Squashed in the back seat of a dually pickup truck, three abreast, Carol and her good friend Melinda Bender did not look forward to the trip home. Earlier, the team leader, Melinda's husband Jack, had decided to make the fourteen-hour trip in a single day. As much as the women had politicked to break the drive into two days, it quickly became apparent who wore the trousers in the Bender family.

Melinda's plea that it would not be a treat for anyone to have two "ill pot," constipated, pre-menopausal women stuffed in the backseat of a truck for that long a period fell on deaf ears as the convoy headed east that Saturday morning. On December 16, with Jack Bender in the lead, and the other workers, including Sam, just behind, the convoy headed out just as the sun broke the horizon in the distance. It was Sam's eighteenth birthday.

The stop for lunch came as a very welcome respite. Prior to the lunch break, stops had lasted only long enough to fill up the vehicle and rush to the bathroom. The crew had decided that this would be a good time to give Sam an impromptu birthday party.

As the group gathered in the corner of a Wendy's and broke into "Happy Birthday," Melinda noticed an older couple watching them. The couple, missing teeth and shabbily dressed, watched with enjoyment as the group, laughed, joked, and sang. They seemed to relish in the moment. As Melinda continued to watch the couple, they seemed to be surrounded in an aura—an aura so bright that it concealed their appearance, an aura that felt warm and happy.

Suddenly, the room grew quiet as the old couple rose and walked over to Sam. The light around them grew brighter as they approached the table and placed a single dollar bill in Sam's hand and wished him a happy birthday. The couple looked as if they did not have a single dollar to spare, yet they gave it to Sam cheerfully. Then, in what seemed like a flash of light, they disappeared, driving away in a rusted old truck.

The story touched me deeply, and I smiled and reached over and touched Carol's hand. "Do you think they might have been angels?"

"Absolutely," she smiled a confident look. "They're around us all the time."

"I hope so," I said.

Carol's brow wrinkled. "You do believe in angels, don't you?"

I shook my head. "I want to. I really want to, but there have been times I've often wondered. There's so very little about them in the Bible and I can't seem to find anyone who can help me put a finger on them or why they're here.

"But, I had a similar experience in the emergency room the time Jane went into a coma. This family appeared to me as if out of nowhere and what drew my attention was an aura that surrounded them. Why they were there remains a mystery to me, but just as they were leaving, the father whispered something to his wife and walked over to me. To this day I cannot remember his words, it was as if he spoke to me through mental telepathy, but I do remember what I felt him saying. He had the kindest eyes and when he placed his hands on my shoulder, for a moment, my fear went away. He assured me that God was with me and that he prayed everything would be all right with my wife. Like the older couple you met on your way back from Mississippi, he and his family disappeared in a flash."

"For years, my favorite TV show was *Touched by an Angel*. I used to tell my friends not to call me on Sunday nights because they'd catch me crying. And my favorite angel was Andrew, the Angel of Death. Rather than being some 'grim reaper' type of guy, Andrew was

207

a loving character, there to help the soul walk from life here on earth into the light of heaven. I pray every day that someone like Andrew was there to take Jane into the light. It sounds to me like Sam has a couple of 'guardian' angels."

I LOVE TO WRITE, and I've found that time soars by me like a rocket into space when I'm writing. An hour passes by like it is only a minute or two. That's what happened to the three hours Carol and I spent at Capt'n Ratty's that day. In the movies, when two actors really connect, they call it chemistry. That's what Bogart and Bacall and Tracy and Hepburn had. That day, there was so much chemistry between Carol and me, that mixed together we could have blown that building to pieces.

I'd never felt like that before in my life. It wasn't the myth of infatuation or that of lust, it was almost electric. Call it passion. Call it love. Call it anything. I will never ever be able to put my finger on it, but all I know is that it was real for me and I knew Carol felt it, too.

Before we left the restaurant, Carol got quiet again—almost pensive. "You don't know how much this has meant to me, Skip."

I lit up like a roman candle, so excited by what she'd said that I missed where she was going. "Well, let's do it again. How about right after Christmas, next Tuesday night I fix you dinner?"

"That would be wonderful," she said, then went back to what she'd planned to tell me before I'd interrupted her. "Skip, I'm so glad we've spent this time together. Actually, I almost called you to postpone our lunch."

"Huh?" I leaned forward. "I—I don't understand."

"Just give me a second," she said. "On the way here, I got a phone call and was told that Billy, Sam's birth father had just died."

Stunned, words left me like the color that rushed from my face. Finally, I asked. "What happened?"

"They said he had a heart attack."

"You okay?" I asked.

"Oh, I'm fine. It's just that I wasn't sure how I was going to tell Sam, I'm not good at things like that. But for some reason, being with you has given me—I don't know what it is, but I feel that it's going to be all right."

"You sure you're okay?"

Carol nodded.

"When's the funeral?" I asked as I helped her with her chair.

"I don't know," she said. "We won't be going."

AS I WALKED CAROL to her car, I again deferred to small talk about Christmas, but with a purpose in mind. Then I sprang it on her. "Would it be okay if I send you some flowers for Christmas?"

"That would be wonderful." She smiled her approval.

I smiled back.

As she opened her car door, Carol lingered a moment then opened another door and I ran right in. "You know, Sam's going to be out of town with a church group for New Years..."

"Really?" I asked.

"Yeah, he'll be with a lot of his friends."

"You planning on doing anything?"

"I guess I'll do like I do every year and bring it in with Dick Clark." Her eyes twinkled.

"Do you think we could? Or maybe you'd like to—" I stuttered.

"Yes, Skip Crayton, I'd love to spend New Year's Eve with you."

As I watched her drive off then cross the bridge that would take her from downtown New Bern, I felt warm inside. I felt connected to Carol. Somehow, I knew that God was leading me in a new direction, and I was ready to follow His lead.

Chapter
53

*T*HE NEXT DAY, I sent Carol a dozen long-stemmed red roses, and then turned my thoughts to the reality that for the first time in more than forty years, I would spend my first Christmas without Jane. With thirty-seven years of marriage, four years in college, and two years in high school, that equaled to almost three-fourths of my lifetime.

I knew that I'd be surrounded by my family and my friends and that God would be with me. I'd made up my mind that I would be a part of Christmas—that with the exception of Jane's absence, very little would change in my Christmas routine.

I'd been a caregiver for much of my married life, and then in the last four years I'd directed all my attention to supporting Jane. Being alone was something new and different for me. I'd never had much time to be alone. But now, for the first time I found myself alone. The strange thing was that I didn't feel lonely. There is a huge difference between the two. It all felt very different. For the first time in my adult life, the only one other than my Little Mutt, that I had to look out for was myself. That was the strangest part.

The week up to Christmas was full. We'd celebrated with my brother's family just before they left for their annual Christmas pilgrimage to Huntington, West

Virginia, to be with Dana's family. I'm sure there were other things that kept me busy, yet I can't remember what they were. I guess the next jolt to my system was wakening on Christmas Eve morning. It was Saturday.

Little Mutt nuzzled up next to me and licked me on the cheek. The sun, already bright, beamed in through my bedroom window letting me know that I'd overslept a little.

At first, I didn't want to get out of bed. I wasn't depressed, just a little pensive. It just felt good laying there next to my dog feeling her love. Shortly, she let me know it was time for her walk.

For most of the United States, Christmas is pictured as a snowy scene with sleigh rides to grandmother's house or bustling shoppers gleefully dodging snowflakes as they finished their last-minute shopping. Christmas in eastern North Carolina is a totally different scene. Sure, we had a white Christmas one year, but most of the time Christmas looked more like that day in 2005. As Little Mutt and I strolled across the golf course with the temperature just breaking sixty-five degrees, golfers were teeing up on the first hole. The blue sky beginning to streak with jet contrails, planes carrying loved ones all across the country, promised a picture perfect "Carolina" Christmas. It was almost as if Jane had painted me another picture.

With my batteries fully charged and my stomach ready for something to eat, I dropped off Little Mutt and walked over to the country club expecting it to be open for breakfast. Disappointed that it was closed, and still hungry, I drove to the Waffle House and slid into the last available table.

Again, God placed me right where he wanted me to be. Before my food arrived, Jerry Pelletier walked up and asked if he could share the booth with me. When I smiled and nodded he sat down. Jerry is a retired

212

surgeon whom I've known for years. Our only association has been social, but he has always been one person I've felt very comfortable being around. That morning, as we ate breakfast I learned more about him than in all the years I've known Jerry. He shared his faith with me. He told me of his trips to the Holy Land. How God had touched his life. In the two hours that we sat together, I found Jerry to be more complete a person than I'd ever thought and, whether he knew it or not, his example and testimony ministered to me that day. I did not realize it at the time, but Jerry was one of the vehicles God was using to speak to me. As I would find out later, angels bring God's messages to us. All we have to do is pay attention and listen. That day, an angel spoke to me through Jerry. When we parted, I knew that Christmas would not be easy—that I'd feel and show deep emotions about the loss of Jane, but that I would get through it and that God would hold my hand.

Chapter
54

CHRISTMAS CAME AND WENT, or maybe it just slipped by like a morning fog melting into the sunlight. I can honestly say that I remember very little of the day or the ones that followed. I know I spent Christmas Eve at my mom's, and I went by Jimmy and Patti's—not that I remember any of it, it's just that's what has always happened and I'm sure it happened that year. Christmas was always such a special time for Jane. She started getting ready months in advance, and as good as my memory usually is, I'm sure that the pain I felt because of her absence that year was much of why things were blocked from my memory. One thing I do remember was how badly I missed Jane. Yet thoughts of Carol played over and over in my mind like a song that will not go away. Finally, on Monday I called to confirm our dinner date.

"How was your Christmas?" I asked.

"It was okay. The tough part was Christmas day over at mom's."

"Yeah, I almost forgot. I guess it was pretty hard on all of you being together for the first time since Michael's death." Carol's nephew Michael had been killed in a car accident that fall and they'd been very close.

"But your flowers helped brighten things up."

"You got them?" I asked.

"Yes, they were beautiful. I love red roses." She sighed. "How'd things go with you?"

"Oh, I got by all right," I said. "Like the song says, I get by with a little help from my friends. And I am truly blessed with my friends and my family. You still on for tomorrow night?" I changed the subject.

"Of course," she answered. "What time?"

"I'll pick you up about six-thirty. You do like ribs, don't you?"

"Skip, my father was a hog farmer. Yes, I like ribs."

"YOU'RE COOKING WHAT?" Jimmy stammered through the phone.

"Ribs," I repeated. "You know how good my ribs are."

"But not on your first date."

"Why?" I asked, a puzzled look on my face.

"They're awkward to eat. You can't just cut them with a knife. You've got to pick them up with your hands and the sauce gets all over the place. It's like fried chicken. The only way is to eat it with your hands."

"Well," I said. "That rules out my second choice."

"How about a good pasta or something?" I could almost hear his head shaking back and forth on the other end.

"No, I've already told her that I'm going to cook ribs and that's what it's going to be. Ribs and collards and fried okra."

"Okay, but I warned you," Jimmy said as he hung up.

I picked Carol up around six and we drove to my house. As soon as we walked in, Little Mutt met us at the back door, her tail wagging back and forth like a kid waving at a new friend. There's something about a dog lover that cannot be faked. It's in their eyes. It's in the way they relate to each other. I could see it in Carol's

215

eyes the first time the two of them met, but now I could see it in Little Mutt. She was truly glad to see Carol again. I knew they'd be fast friends.

Dinner was flawless and I told Carol how Jimmy had warned me about the ribs. I also found out that cooking was not one of Carol's fortes and that she really appreciated my skill in the kitchen. After we cleared the table, we returned to the family room to talk and listen to some music. I had the entire Rod Stewart's "Standards" collection and put a CD into the player. That night, we shared more stories about ourselves and found bonds we never knew existed. We held hands and spent quiet moments just looking at one another, drinking in the atmosphere. That night, we never kissed. But she looked at me with eyes so dreamy, I felt she could eat me alive.

To say that the evening flew by would be like an unbelievable cliché, yet in what seemed only minutes, midnight arrived before we both knew it. On the way back to her house, Carol insisted that Little Mutt go with us, a ritual that would repeat itself over and over again in the months ahead.

As I walked Carol to her door, she leaned against me and placed her arm around my waist. "I had a wonderful time," she said. "Be sure and tell Jimmy how much I liked the ribs."

Chuckling, I answered, "I will."

As we stood at her door, the awkward moment led to a long silence. *Do I try to kiss her,* I asked myself. *No, don't push things. Remember, she wants to take things a little slow.* But before I said good night, I extended our awkward moment by leaning over and kissing her on the cheek.

"I really had a good time, too," I said as I turned to walk back to the car, hoping she'd let the kiss slide by. "I'm looking forward to Saturday."

Before I reached my car, Carol called back. "What time?"

Again my inexperience in dating made for another blushing moment. "Oh yeah. I've got to go to Kenly to my cousin's wedding. I'll be back in time to pick you up by six. I've lined up a driver. We'll go by Jimmy and Patti's for a drink, then head to the beach for dinner."

"I'm really looking forward to it," she said. "That was our first kiss you know."

I don't think I drove home that night. I think I floated home.

Chapter 55

*M*Y COUSIN'S WEDDING was scheduled for New Year's Eve Day in Kenly, a town about an hour and a half west of New Bern. Jane and I had always been fairly slack about attending family functions, especially on my side of the family. That changed after her coma as we both realized that there were cousins and family we'd both never gotten to know.

One of the best times we had was at a family reunion with Jane's cousins on her mother's side, an event we'd vowed not to miss in the future. We both realized how important extended family is. We made a promise to each other to focus more on both our families. I made a pact with myself to keep that promise even after Jane's death.

Carol and I had started emailing one another. The day before, she'd sent me an email that told me she shared my excitement about our upcoming date.

Would have called but thought you might be taking a nap... haven't got a whole lot accomplished today but I tried and that should count for something ... am going to a movie and out to eat with some heathen girlfriends (actually they are all church friends) ... please pray for our teens traveling to Lynchburg VA ... Sam is riding with Andrew and although he is a good driver, I'm a little nervous ... spoke with him a few minutes ago and they were in Danville ... I am really looking forward to tomorrow evening ... IF IT EVER GETS HERE..."

I AWOKE New Year's Eve morning and dashed to my computer. I had not talked to Carol the night before and hoped I'd find a message. Little Mutt would have to wait for her morning walk. As I opened my email, I smiled when I saw her name. The message had been sent at 4:58 a.m.

I do hope that you are still asleep ... I am happily typing away and trying to play catch up on my work since I have been such a slacker this week.... Have scanned the morning paper (I am so thankful that it is delivered around 4 a.m.) Ate some yogurt for breakfast and am hard at work... Hope I can catch a quick nap this afternoon so I can last to the wee hours tonight. Had a great time last night with the girls (mixed emotions about the movie) but it was a nice relaxing time... Hope you had a great evening as well... looking forward to your morning email... you are such an uplifting person.

I quickly emailed her back and told her that I could not wait to pick her up.

With anxious feelings, I set out for Kenly that morning. The excitement of going out with Carol almost overwhelmed me and the further west I drove, the more anxious I felt—like little fingers dancing across my face and chest. My heart was not on the trip with me, but waiting for me back home, and all I could think of was getting the wedding over and heading back to New Bern.

I've found over the years that when my heart is not in the right place, God reaches down and puts it where He wants it to be. As I sat in the church struggling to focus on the beauty and simplicity of the wedding, something drew me to what I call the challenge to the couple. I guess I'd been to at least a hundred wedding ceremonies and, with little variation, they'd all seemed pretty much the same. This time, the minister caught my attention as if his message had been directed solely at me. He referred to God's mystery of taking two people, a man and a woman from two unrelated families and creating, through their marriage and love to one another, a bond—one that exceeds that of parent and child or brother and sister. It was as if I'd been struck by lightning. I'd never thought about that bond. At that moment I realized that I'd been blessed with that bond before, and I wondered if I could ever be blessed with something so precious again. Thoughts of what that minister had said stayed with me as I drove home, replacing any anxiety that had been there before. And again I heard the angel speaking God's message to me through that minister. For the first time in my life, I was beginning to pay attention.

I GUESS I'D BEEN DRESSED an hour or more before I saw Jimmy's van turn into my driveway. Used for special occasions and football trips, Jimmy's custom Chevy Van was perfect for the excursion we'd planned. I watched through the foyer windows as the driver, an affable man by the name of Curtis, parked the van and strolled to my front porch. Before he could knock on the door I opened it.

"Good evening, Mr. Crayton. Your ride is here."

"What's happening Curtis?" I said. "I'll meet you at the van. I just need to say goodbye to my little girl and lock up."

Curtis tipped his hat and left the porch as I went back into the family room to let Little Mutt know that I'd be back. Ever since Jane's death, it seemed important for me to let her know that I'd be back— something I'd say over and over to her. Yet each time I left, her sadness at my leaving followed me out the door. As I reached the couch, she spoke through her eyes. Stretched out on the couch in her "dust mop pose," Little Mutt raised her eyebrows and pleaded to me not to leave.

"I'll be back," I promised. "And maybe the nice lady Carol will be with me."

Her tail popped up and began to tick-tock back and forth in her effort to let me know that she understood, but her eyes never changed.

"I promise," I said again. "I'll be back."

Chapter
56

ON THE RIDE out to Carol's house, I sat up front with Curtis. As we turned onto the road where she lived, another sunset grabbed my attention. Unlike the consoling one at the creek full of blues, purples, and golds, this afterglow startled my senses with the most brilliant reds I'd ever seen, highlighted by oranges and golds. It was as if that sunset Jane painted for me at the creek had been her assurance to me that life after death was truly hers. This brilliant spectacle seemed to announce that I was about to enter a new life—that indeed, there was going to be life after her death for me. A feeling of joy covered me like a warm blanket on a cold night.

Today when young people date, they either meet some place or "hang out" together. When my generation dated, the proper thing for a guy to do was to pick up his date at her house. Knocking on Carol's door took me back more than forty years. Yet, it somehow felt right. And when she appeared at the door, the radiance in her smile sent my cautioned excitement into high gear. I couldn't wait for her to meet Patti and Jimmy.

"You look wonderful," I said as she pulled the door to. "Right this way, your carriage awaits you."

The ride to Jimmy's house was more like a flight on a magic carpet. It was as if we'd been sprinkled with fairy dust as Captain Curtis piloted our flying galleon to Never-Never Land. Within moments, we turned into the drive and "landed" at Jimmy's front door.

"Nervous?" I asked as I offered Carol my hand.

"Just a little." She smiled a faint smile. "You know you take me far from my comfort zone."

"Good. That's what I want to do. I want to take you to places you've only dreamed about. I want to show you off to everyone I know."

Carol's smile widened. "You sound like I'm someone special. I'm just a country girl from Spring Garden."

"Well, that's all I am." I gently led her to the front door.

She stopped and turned me toward her, an infectious twinkle in her eye. "What? You? A country boy? You never even knew there were any other high schools in Craven County other than New Bern and Havelock."

"Sure, I'm a country boy—as good as it gets." I tilted my head and smiled.

"Huh?" a confused Carol asked.

"Carol, I grew up right next to the country club. You can't get any more country than that." We were both still laughing when we walked into the foyer of Jimmy's house.

Patti and Jimmy welcomed us and led us into the family room and offered us a glass of wine. Always gracious, my two best friends are not the least bit pretentious. They are warm giving people who easily make those around them comfortable and to feel at home. And to those who share time with them, it becomes quickly recognizable that their welcome is genuine and not contrived. Their warmth is contagious, and I immediately saw Carol accepting the friendship that they so openly offered. Within moments it was as if Carol and Patti had known each other for years. Watching them get to know one another, Jimmy and I smiled at each other. I knew what I was seeing would be as Paul Henreid said to Humphrey Bogart in the last scene of *Casablanca*, "This is the beginning of a beautiful friendship."

Chapter
57

*A*T EIGHT O'CLOCK SHARP, our driver Curtis let us out at the front door of my favorite Atlantic Beach café, The Island Grill. Within seconds the four of us were whisked to our booth and menus placed in front of us. The ride to the beach was fun, and the fun continued through dinner.

As we left the restaurant I asked Carol, "Well, what did you think?"

"Skip, to be completely honest with you," she grabbed my hand and squeezed it, "when we first pulled up, I thought to myself, 'where in the world is he taking me?' I figured we'd be eating hot dogs with lukewarm beer. Boy, was I surprised."

I squeezed her hand back and laughed. "Yeah, kinda like the old 'judging a book by its cover' thing. Now I want to take you to one of my favorite places in the world."

WITH PATTI AND JIMMY already onboard, Curtis pulled the van up and motioned for us to get inside. "Tell Jimmy we're going to walk. I'll see them at the house," I said as I closed the door to the van.

As the van turned onto East Boardwalk and headed down the road that ran next to the ocean, Carol and I strolled along behind holding hands. "I guess this favorite place of yours is not far?" Carol asked.

"Just up the street," I said.

"And why is this place so special?" Carol changed hands, put her arm through mine, and pulled closer.

"You remember the farewell column I wrote about Jane in the Sun Journal?" Carol felt good against my side. She didn't know it, but I was already falling in love with her.

"I think everybody in New Bern remembers that one. It was so special, anyone who read it and didn't shed at least one tear doesn't know how to feel." She looked up at me, her eyes soft and warm.

"Well, just up the street is our beach house." In the column, I had written of how a certain stretch of sand had held so many memories for me, how the beach had been a part of so many of my triumphs and losses. You remember the stretch of sand that I wrote about? I'm going to take you there."

By the time we reached the house, Jimmy and Patti were already inside listening to music. I quickly showed Carol around then grabbed her hand and led her to the front porch. The night was "Chamber of Commerce" perfect with a full moon glistening against the gentle waves as they slowly kissed the beach—just cool enough for me to take Carol into my arms.

For a moment, we just stood on the porch taking in the majesty of what nature was presenting as if we were the only ones in the audience. Slowly, I moved closer to her and looked into her eyes.

"Carol," I started. "This is my special place, that stretch of sand that has been so much a part of my most important memories. I will never be able to close that book, written by those memories. But tonight I want to begin another chapter; a chapter that includes you in my life." I gently pulled Carol into my arms and kissed her. And she kissed me back.

We stood there looking into each other's eyes. Finally, she spoke. "Skip, I want so much to be a part of your

225

life, to help write another chapter that will include me and Sam, but a part of me is afraid. I pray that it is a fear that I can overcome if you'll lead me."

"All I want us to do is to try," I said.

"And there is one other thing," she said. "If we're going to try, I want to do it right with you. I need your promise that we will not be going to bed with each other."

"You mean going all the way?" I laughed.

"Seriously." Her eyes showed her determination. "Kissing and touching is okay, but not the rest."

"That's cool with me," I smiled. "I waited for six years the first time."

Carol stepped back. "You mean that you and Jane...?"

"That's right. The first time was on our wedding night. It was an understanding we both had. We waited six years before we did it, and we lasted thirty-seven years."

As we turned to walk inside, Carol wrapped her arm around me. "You never cease to amaze me, Mr. Crayton."

Carol and I dropped off Jimmy and Patti just before midnight and went to my house to bring in the New Year together. Later, when I awoke our driver and began helping him scrape the ice from the windshield, I looked at my watch. It was 2:15 a.m. I'm sure it had been at least fifteen years since I'd been up that late, but I didn't feel tired. Elation, that's what I felt. It was as if the smile that had been lying dormant in me for so long was about to break through. I felt like a distant sun was rising within me—a light that had not surfaced in years. Euphoria slowly crept over me like being at the birth of your first child. For the first time since Jane got sick some four years before, I started to feel and it felt wonderful.

As we drove Carol to her house, we talked about the adventure that lay before us: getting to know one another. One thing that stood out most for me was something that Carol said just before we reached her house. "Skip, if something is going to happen between us, it will be a gift from God, and it will be right. You see, He never makes mistakes."

After a "real" kiss goodnight, Curtis drove the carriage and its prince back to the castle. As I opened the back door to my house and walked past my office, the urge to leave one last message for Carol to wake up to overwhelmed me. So, I quickly opened my email and told her how magical the night had been.

Still high on the evening, I scooped up Little Mutt, took her upstairs, tucked her into bed beside me and waited for sleep to take over, praying that I would not awaken in the morning only to find a glass slipper.

Chapter 58

*T*HUS BEGAN the longest eight-week courtship in the history of modern romance. We had agreed to take things easy and slowly build our relationship. Yet what seemed to be unfolding at a crawl for both of us, as I look back, was almost lightning fast. I was already falling all over myself for Carol and I hadn't even met Sam.

Older couples fall in love with each other all the time only to be burdened by family, especially kids. Lots of times, the kids are the ones who put up the real block to a relationship either through allegiances to another parent or, in the case of an older boy, protecting his mother, or just resisting the fact that someone new might come into their lives creating change. Divorce can be especially devastating on kids. In our ever-selfish "me" generation, parents oftentimes never really notice the real victims of a "broken" marriage until it's too late.

I hoped that those pitfalls would not affect us. I did not have children, and Sam's dad, who had not been a daily fixture in his life, had died. I did have Debbie and Glenn, my niece and nephew who Jane and I had helped raise, but they were not my kids and I had this strange hunch that they'd be my first line of support if ever anything happened between Carol and me.

But Sam could have easily been a "juvenile delinquent" or a spoiled brat. He could have been one of those kids who would resist my efforts, because as surrogate "man of the house," he wanted to protect his mom. I guess he could have also been complacent, looking at me as a mild interruption in his lifestyle, like a common cold that, if endured long enough, would eventually go away. Sam was none of the above.

When I finally met Sam, to use a really worn-out cliché, I was blown away. I did not get a "juvenile delinquent." What I did get in Sam was a six-foot-two honor student with GQ good looks, a member of the high school golf team with an academic scholarship to Campbell University; a young man with a smile so warm that it would instantly bring ice water to a boil.

It took only moments for me to realize how much we had in common. We both loved college football and conservative politics, and shared the same theology. For both of us, the bond was immediate, and right then and there I felt God's presence in all our lives. If I had placed an order with God for a son, he'd have sent me Samuel Jackson Dail.

We became instant friends. I quickly learned that Sam and I were so much alike that we even had the propensity of spilling things on our shirts when we ate. Our first time together was a dinner that he and I were going to cook for Carol. Also like me, Sam likes to cook and enjoys trying different things. He is always the first one when we eat out to ask our waiter about the restaurant's specialty and to order it. I do believe he'd try buffalo chips if the café boasted it as a specialty.

The only thing that I remember from our menu that night was that we started with calamari, and Sam became an instant fan. If it's available on a menu as a starter, he is always one to order it. I can also remember that after dinner, when Sam left to pick up his date for the movie that night, I felt that a huge hurdle in my quest for Carol had been cleared. Carol's smiling face told me that the evening had not just been

229

successful, but that it had become the beginning of a long and close friendship. I knew that what had started that night would create a lasting bond between the two of us. But I had no clue how special that relationship would become.

That evening, as Carol and I sat on the couch listening to Rod Stewart, I made it clear that if anything bloomed between the two of us, that I would happily take a back seat to Sam. I'd never make her choose between the two of us.

For a time, she got very quiet. I'd wondered if I'd put too much pressure on her regarding me and Sam. "Did I say something wrong?" I asked.

She placed her hand on my shoulder and looked into my eyes. "No. Not at all. Seeing the two of you together is just another one of the dreams I've had recently that has all of a sudden come true. As much as I've dreamed of Sam going off to college, I've dreaded August 17."

"August 17?" I asked.

"Yeah. That's the day I've got to take Sam to Campbell. I know I am going to be a basket case. The thought of coming home to my house all by myself for the first time in eighteen years scares me to death."

"I'll be with you, if you want," I assured her.

"I knew you'd say that. If that day does come and you are there, I can assure you that you and Sam will share the stage of my life together."

Chapter
59

*U*NLIKE the "hanging out" kids do together when they date, things were different when I was coming along. Back then, almost all dating took place exclusively at the girl's home. Today, that is different, but in a good way. Because the kids hang out at each other's homes, they quickly become familiar with each other's parents. And now, a new Jane was about to enter my life.

Carol and I, being from the "old school" of dating, went about our daily routine of seeing each other in the familiar fashion of me driving to her house in Spring Garden—a community about fifteen minutes away—picking Carol up, going on our date, which usually finished at my house, then Little Mutt and I taking her home around midnight.

One particular evening, as I arrived at Carol's house, I noticed another car in her driveway. Now another car in Carol's drive was not really something that would bring up any sinister suspicion. I think that Carol might be related to every single resident that lives in western Craven County, so another car being at her house could have been anybody.

As I knocked on Carol's side door, I was not met by Carol, but by this most ravishing creature by the name of Jane Moon. "Hi, my name is Jane Moon," she said as she opened the door. "I'm Sam's girlfriend."

231

Carol had told me about Jane when I met Sam, but I had no clue that she would be so gorgeous. She is as beautiful as a morning sunrise and as breathtaking as a mountain waterfall. Her long, jet-black hair shimmers like a full moon rising through late-night clouds. But the single thing that makes Jane so special is that she is kind to a fault and very comfortable in her own skin. Jane is about five-foot-four inches tall with a figure that a model would envy. She is Korean–American and one of my first thoughts shortly after I met her was that she and Sam, if they ever married, would have some great-looking kids.

Jane and Sam had been together for almost two years and there was another thing that I noticed about their relationship. They acted more like a couple that had been married for many years. They seemed comfortable with each other. So many times early teenager infatuation is just that: infatuation. What I noticed was a mature, giving relationship, in that they did not smother one another, yet allowed each other the freedom to be themselves. They did not have to be together every waking hour, yet when they were together they seemed to really enjoy the time that they shared. Few couples ever share what Sam and Jane seemed to have.

That night I had brought pizza and a movie. After the four of us ate, we settled in to watch one of my favorites, "Sea Biscuit." Carol and I took the couch, and Sam and Jane sat on the floor in front of us. Not having kids, I'd never paid much attention to movie ratings. I usually watched what I liked. Things really clipped along as we all sat and enjoyed the movie, then came the scene in the brothel. The hair on my arm stood at attention as I recalled the scene with its partial nudity. Before I could reach for the remote, the hooker quickly revealed a breast. In my embarrassment, I looked over at Carol and mouthed, "I'm sorry." Carol smiled back and mouthed, "Don't worry about it." The kids never missed a beat. That was my first lesson in parenthood.

Chapter 60

*A*S WE *SLOWLY* MOVED FORWARD in our relationship, the month of January was not quite half over, but to us both the days and weeks had lasted a lifetime. We were well on our way to getting to know each other, and I knew that I was passionately in *love* with Carol. And I knew Carol was in *love* with me, but to get her to say that one four letter word I so desperately wanted to hear was close to impossible.

Carol had been hurt so much in previous relationships that giving her heart completely was something that she feared. Twice she'd been jilted and once, after getting engaged, she ended it. Marriage was such a painful word to her that she never attended weddings. She told me that there was a fence around her heart that protected her, that's when I started carrying wire cutters.

"I'm a patient man," I told Carol. "I'll just cut that fence away, piece by piece."

Things were happening in my life that I did not understand. My Jane had been gone less than six months and here I was falling in love with someone else. It wasn't just that my love for Jane had diminished in any way, it was just that Carol had come into my life so unexpectedly. There had been others who'd made overtures or offered favor my way, all attractive and available, but none had been of any interest to me. I had not been single or uncommitted for more than forty years and it was a state of mind that I was actually enjoying.

And there was one other thing. I really don't care what political correctness indicates, Southerners are different from any other culture in America. I am a Southerner and so are my family and most of my friends. Because of that heritage, I had entered into what the southern culture called "my time of mourning," a period that most Southerners expect should last at least a year.

But things changed when God placed Carol in my life. I was and am still convinced to this day that He sent her to me. Not one time in our courtship did I ever feel guilty or like I was cheating on Jane. I didn't care what my friends or family expected from me. I had finally realized that it was *my* life and I was not going to let others dictate what I was going to do with it. I was turning sixty in May, and I wanted to do it my way. Other than Carol and God, no one else had a vote. I knew that things were as they were supposed to be.

And while I didn't know it, Carol was experiencing similar feelings. She told me later that for years she'd prayed that God would one day place the man He wanted her to spend the rest of her life with squarely on her front porch. After years of praying that particular prayer, one day she changed it.

She said to God, "If You have someone in mind for me, You'll do it in Your way and in Your time, not mine." In God's wonderful sense of humor, instead of placing someone on Carol's porch, He placed her on mine the night of the ball.

Still, she had been reluctant to speak those three words I so longed to hear her say. As badly I wanted to hear them, I did not push. I just kept snipping away at that fence. Snips need to be subtle, like watching a

235

sunset before Wednesday night communion, or bringing a single rose, or a dozen, or two, or three. An email in the evening and one to wake her up, copying songs or just catching her in traffic and taking her to lunch. I guess some might call it persistence, but persistence doesn't make someone fall in love. The little snips are the subtle steps that caress a loving heart and lets it know that it is okay to say the words. God had told me to snip away at that fence, and I was following His lead. I knew that when God was ready for her to say those words, He would tell her when the time was right.

On a warm Monday in late January as we sat on a bench at Union Point in downtown New Bern gazing at the river, Carol turned me to her. Her eyes met mine and without hesitation she said, "Mr. Crayton, I'm madly in love with you."

Chapter
61

I THINK IT WAS A FRIDAY when I asked Carol to marry me. I don't remember the exact day, but it was sometime near the end of January. I had not gotten down on a knee and produced a ring yet and I'm not sure that I really asked her. It may have come up in mutual discussion. But one thing was for sure: we planned to get married.

One night as Little Mutt and I were driving Carol home, I mentioned that it might be nice to shoot for December, and since the tenth would be the anniversary of our first "non-date," that December 10 might be a perfect date. It would give us additional time to get to know one another and Sam the time to become better acquainted with me. In the back of my mind, although I never admitted it, it would also take place more than a year after Jane's death therefore appeasing those friends and family trapped within their Southern upbringing.

As we approached a stoplight, Carol sat quietly musing upon my suggestion. Just as the stoplight changed and I brought the car up to speed, Carol said, "I was thinking about maybe April or May." Surprised at what she said, I ran off the road. Again.

I gulped and glanced over at Carol. "Sure, baby. That sounds great to me. I'd do it tonight."

Before I asked the reason, Carol continued. "Skip, we're in love. We both know that, so it really doesn't matter when we get married. But, I was thinking about Sam. He's crazy about you. Jane says you're all he talks about. I want us to build our family, the three of us, before he goes off to college. I want him to have his own bedroom in our house, his home. I want that home to be the place he comes back to at Thanksgiving, Christmas, and summers. If we get married after he goes off to school, he will have already established some sort of home somewhere else. I want his home to be with us."

My heart swelled to overflowing. What Carol had just said made mountains of sense. I knew without question that it would be the right thing to do. It was not just the right thing, it was what I wanted to do. That night on the way to what would soon "not" be Carol's house anymore, I took another step toward becoming a parent, and I loved every moment of it.

A few days later, I arrived early at Carol's house. I had asked to speak to Sam before Carol and I went out to dinner. He and Carol had been in Raleigh picking up his graduation present, a "school bus-yellow" Land Rover Discovery. That day, she had prepared Sam for my reason to meet with him. When he heard what she'd had to say, he, too, ran off the road.

Sam greeted me at the door and I asked him to meet with me alone in the living room. As we both sat down I told him that for my generation there was a Southern tradition that when a man asks for a woman's hand in marriage, he first would have to ask the woman's father for permission.

"Sam, your grandfather is not with us anymore, therefore you will need to take his place." I took a deep breath. "Sam, I want your permission to ask your mother to marry me."

For a moment Sam sat quietly. As the moment slipped into an awkward silence, I noticed Sam shift back and forth and finally look over his shoulder. Next I watched as a sheepish grin crossed his face.

"Mother, I can't do it," he said. "Yes, yes you can marry my mother."

My mouth dropped when I heard Carol's laugh as she entered the room. "It's okay, Sam," she said. "Skip, we were going to play a little trick on you, but it appears Sam didn't want to break your heart, even if only for a second. We'd planned for him to say 'no' but it appears that my son could not go through with it."

My heart pounded as I reached over, grabbed Sam's hand and shook it. I reached for Carol and pulled the three of us together, the beginning of my new family.

Chapter 62

*J*IMMY AND PATTI were the first ones who knew that Carol and I planned to marry. In my family, the first person to know was my mother. Telling her, I thought, would be a very interesting experience. Her response to my announcement could have been as varied as shock, amusement, or encouragement. Asking her to keep my secret until it had become official with a ring and all would also be interesting. On one hand, Flossie could choose to abide by my wishes, while on the other, I might as well place an ad on the front page of our daily newspaper.

Another reaction was also possible. Remember that Southern culture thing? What other people think has been a driving force for my mother most of her life, and she learned early on how to guilt her children with the best of them. For years I'd called her "Lila" behind her back after the manipulative mother in Pat Conroy's novel *The Prince of Tides.*

Fortunately, some years before, with the help of a wonderful therapist, I'd learned to dodge my mother's arrows of guilt and ignore them. Oddly enough, that's when Flossie started to respect me. After a couple of years of trying to manipulate me the old fashion way, she finally gave up.

But still, Flossie was a product of her upbringing, and I had prepared myself for the worst. Again, she surprised me.

"I know that you loved Jane very much and that the two of you shared many wonderful years together." My eyes widened as she continued. "You were a good husband to her, especially in her time of need, and I know that she would agree with me that you should not be lonely for the rest of your life. Carol is that person. I can see in her eyes that she loves you and I know that you love her. It would be a shame for you to let her go. She is the right person for this time in your life."

I took a deep breath. I had not expected that from Flossie. I had actually briefed myself and was prepared to bring my case to the court of motherly approval. Then she surprised me again. "Tell me about Sam."

"Mom," I beamed. "He is so special. He is the son I never had. Carol has done such a great job raising him."

"I'm glad for all of you," she said. Then she changed the subject again. "Have y'all picked out a ring?"

"Not yet. I want to do that myself," I said. "I really want to surprise Carol so I'll probably start looking today or tomorrow."

"Excuse me," she said as she got up and left the room. Perplexed, I could hear her upstairs rummaging through drawers. A few minutes later she came back downstairs with a small bag in her hand. She handed it to me and sat back down.

I stared at the bag, having no idea what was inside. My eyes asked the question.

"You know how your father loved to buy jewelry?" she began. "One time when he was in Amsterdam, he came upon the stones that are in that bag in hopes that one day someone in our family might use them to make a ring. I think the timing is right. If you like them, I'd be

241

honored if you'll use them as a gift to Carol from your father and me."

In my entire life the only thing I could ever remember my mother giving me was a pair of Bass Weejuns when I was fourteen years old. And now, what I discovered in that bag were five perfectly matched diamonds—one large one, and four small ones each the same cut, color and clarity.

Chapter
63

ELLING MY SISTER DEBBY I was getting married was never an issue. Neither of us has ever been able to recall when I told her that Carol and I were getting married. I do remember Debby saying that as happy as she was for us, she would always love Jane and hold her memory close to her heart. In no way was any of that anything less than positive to Carol or me.

The next hurdle I had to face was my brother Frank and his wife Dana. Frank and I were on our way to Jacksonville, North Carolina for a meeting when I dropped the bomb on him. Startled, he also ran off the road. A quick call to his wife Dana and the hesitation in her voice told me that this hurdle would not be an easy one to cross. My brother and his wife are great parents. They have raised two outstanding kids, Walt and Anna. They also hold Southern culture to its highest regard.

The fact that Carol and I had even announced that we were getting engaged was for them, as I perceived it, a social "no-no." I have always been pretty good at spotting insincerity, and as nice as they both tried to be, it was all over their voices.

Yet for all they'd tried to ingest as I blindsided them with my announcement, I honestly feel that Frank and Dana had my best interest at heart. Think about it. They hardly knew Carol. Jane, whom they'd known most of their lives and who'd been an integral part of our family, had been dead for less than six months, and now I'm planning to get married in the spring. I'm sure they had trouble coming to terms with my decision. They wanted to make sure that I did not fall for the very first person who'd paid me any attention.

What they didn't comprehend was that it was the other way around. It was Carol who had the most to lose. I had been the aggressor, the one who diligently snipped away at the fence around her heart. And then there was God. I knew beyond a shadow of a doubt He had brought us together, and He never makes mistakes.

At least they were positive around me and didn't try to convince me to wait; an effort that they were smart enough to have realized would have been futile. If they made comments to the contrary behind my back, I never heard them, and in reality, I wouldn't have cared. The only ones who had a vote were Carol, Sam, and me. And of course God.

Telling Debbie and Glenn was altogether different. Debbie and Glenn's father had been an only child, and Jane and I were their only aunt and uncle. When their mother died, Debbie was eleven and Glenn was four. Jane became a sort of surrogate mother to them both, even after their father remarried. We were very much a part of their lives and they both spent huge amounts of time with us. They spent at least two weekends a month with us, stayed with us at the beach, and went on trips with us. In turn, we were there with them for Cub Scout meetings, school graduations, Junior-Miss pageants, football games, and on and on. I had mixed feelings about calling them.

After Jimmy's first wife Louise died, he and Patti married some five months later. At first, there was friction from Jimmy's kids. For the most part, his son immediately accepted the marriage, but his two daughters were somewhat reluctant. Although they both tried to hide the reluctance from both Jimmy and Patti, they turned to Jane with their questions and fears. Fortunately for the girls, Jane, who was a very close friend to both Patti and Louise, was able to minister to those two girls in a way that helped them to accept the union. Today, they are big fans of Patti and share their lives with her.

I wanted a smooth transition with Glenn and Debbie. I had worked side by side with Glenn for more than four years, and I had an idea that he and his wife Christine would be supportive, so I decided to call him first. When I told him of the upcoming nuptials, I had to hold the phone away from my ear. "Hey, Christine! Skip's getting married. Halleluiah!"

Christine grabbed the phone and said, "Tell me it's the Carol we've been hearing about. I've heard she is wonderful."

"She's the one," I said.

"We've been so worried about you," Christine said. "You were so sad at Christmas. When's the wedding?"

When I finished the call, I took a deep breath and stepped from the cloud I'd been walking on back to the floor and called Debbie.

Debbie Stilley Williams, unlike Glenn, is a deep thinker, a ponderer. She does not make quick decisions. Debbie has to weigh all that is laid in front of her and, therefore, I didn't expect a similar reaction.

When she answered, I began with small talk then I lit the match. "Debbie, you know I've been seeing someone—"

"And you've asked her to marry you," she interrupted. "Haven't you?"

"Yes."

"I knew that's what you were going to say. I just knew it," her voice pitching an octave higher. "I knew it would happen someday, but I didn't think it would be this soon."

"So?" I asked, caution in my voice.

"I've got to have time to think," she said. "Oh, I'm not mad or anything, it's just that I've got to think...you know me."

"Yes, Debbie, I do know you. You are my steadfast one. You take all the time you need and call me."

"Okay, Skip. I love you."

"I love you, too," I said as I heard the phone click.

I'd pretty much gotten the results I'd expected. Had my daughter Mary Ruth lived, she would have probably hung up on me, but Jane was her mother. Or maybe she'd have turned to Patti for guidance. But either way, neither she nor Glenn, nor Debbie, nor anyone else had a say in this one. It was a done deal.

Two days later I got a call from Debbie Stilley. "Skip, I'm so happy for you. When can we meet Carol?"

DEBBIE WOULD LATER TELL ME that during her pondering she recalled when her own mother had died. Her father had remarried four months later, a marriage that had lasted for more than thirty years. She also remembered the reaction of Jane and her grandparents at that marriage, that old Southern culture rearing its ugly head. She reminded me of how her stepmother had been a real mother to her and her brother. Debbie said that she knew that Carol and I were doing the right thing.

Chapter
64

INALLY, the pot was right. We'd taken care of my side of the family. Now it was time to meet face-to-face with Carol's oldest brother Merril Jr. and his wife Bridgett, our two biggest supporters. We'd been invited to attend Carol's nephew's baptism in Raleigh. Being raised a Methodist, dunking had always fascinated me and so I looked forward to the event.

I met Carol at her mother's house. With Sam and Jane in the front seat and Carol, her mom, and I in the back, we motored toward Raleigh in Sam's new truck. Unfortunately, when we got to the church, we were informed that the Baptism was being postponed. Someone had forgotten to heat up the water in the Baptismal. Somehow John never had to deal with that problem in the Jordan.

Meeting Merril and Bridgett was a real joy. Often, it's impossible to place a face on a voice, but the two of them looked just the way I'd imagined—Merril, just a few months younger than I, about six-one, lean with dark hair and a prankster personality; Bridgett, a tall woman with silky shoulder length hair that framed her bright eyes and huge smile. I took to both immediately. When Bridgett asked me about the ring, which was now

247

being set, she started to cry as I described it to her. I wonder if the tears in my eyes had anything to do with her emotions.

After church, we all gathered at a barbecue restaurant with the rest of Merril and Bridgett's family. I got the impression that the baptism was not the main reason for the get-together. It was time for them all to take a look at Skip.

After lunch, back at Merril's cozy home in North Raleigh, I felt as if I'd been a member of this wonderful family my whole life. I knew that I fit in. Unlike the convincing I had to do with my family, the Dail family accepted me at face value. For them, I could have been a garbage man or a street sweeper and it would not have mattered. The mere fact that I loved Carol and Sam was all it took.

I really knew that I was onboard when the family sparring started. Just because I was new, I was not spared from Merril's jokes and pranks, yet one thing he said got my attention...*It really got my attention.*

In a toast to Carol and me, Merril said, "My best to you, Skip. Carol is a wonderful sister and will make you a wonderful wife...if she makes it to the wedding."

His toast was followed by laughter. I cocked my head and gazed at him in confusion. "What?"

"Oh, didn't you know?" he continued with a faint smile. "Carol has a tendency of not making it down the aisle."

I raised my glass back to Merril and said something like: "This time will be different." But his remark bothered me on the way home and for several days after until I buried it behind my huge desire for Carol. Unfortunately, his remark would raise its head again.

Chapter 65

WHEN CAROL AND I first started dating, I had already made plans to go to a real estate convention in San Francisco the first week of February. When my cousin Fred and his wife Bea heard I was going to be there, they told me that they would also be in the area. They suggested I go out a few days early so we could spend some time in Napa. One of his friends, when he heard that Fred would be spending a few days in wine country, told Fred that sending him to Napa would be like sending Liberace to Boy's Town.

The two places in the world Carol had always wanted to visit were Napa Valley and Tuscany. I'd made plans with my sister to go to Italy that spring, but placed that one on hold when Carol and I got engaged.

Early in our dating, I'd asked Carol to go with me to Napa, but she declined. Her "heathen" girlfriends, a group of gals from the Baptist church, had warned her against going. This group of women, acting as "mother hens," had put their protective armor around Carol, suggesting that it would not be proper as she might come away from the trip feeling hurt and abused. After we got engaged, those same girlfriends changed their minds and urged Carol to go with me. I love my Southern roots, but sometimes the "rules" can be ridiculous.

249

On the night Carol and I got "officially" engaged, I'd met Sam in the afternoon to show him the ring. As I paced the parking lot at the place where I'd told Sam to meet me, I must have looked at my watch a dozen times. I desperately wanted his approval. When he finally arrived right on time, he pulled his truck up next to my car and before he could put it in park, I had yanked open the passenger door and shoved the box into his hand. As he opened it, his eyes lit up.

"Well?" I stuffed both shaking hands into my pockets. "What do you think?"

Sam showed his approval with a genuine smile and a nod. "She is going to love it." When he shook my hand, I knew I had his blessing.

Later that evening as Carol and I headed to my house with the ring box in my pocket, I felt like an over-filled balloon, afraid that the smallest bump in the road would have made me pop. Carol acted as if nothing special was happening, but I knew that she knew one night I'd officially ask the question.

When we walked into the kitchen, I could not go any further and dropped to one knee, popped open the box and asked, "Will you marry me?"

Carol smiled as I fumbled with the ring, "Yes, Skip Crayton. I will marry you. I love you with all my heart."

I placed the ring on Carol's finger. She slowly raised her hand in front of her. "Gosh," she said. "I never expected anything like this. Skip, this is so beautiful. Where did you find it?"

"I had it made," I beamed. "My dad picked out the diamonds."

"Your dad?"

"Long story," I said. "I'll tell you about it at dinner. Let's go show it to Jimmy and Patti."

"Not yet, big boy." Carol's face softened, her eyes moist and dreamy. "Right now I want a hug and a kiss."

THAT NIGHT our magical journey continued. When we walked into Jimmy's house, we were greeted by a huge congratulations banner strung across the foyer. After a glass of wine, the four of us went out to one of our favorite restaurants where the owner comped the entire meal. That night, we had been sprinkled with "fairy dust."

After dinner as we drove back to Carol's house, she brought up Napa. "You're leaving for California what day next week?"

Wondering why that subject had come up, I glanced over at her. "I'm leaving a week from next Thursday. I plan to spend one night in San Francisco, meet my cousin, then go to Napa for Friday night and Saturday night and return to the city on Sunday for the convention."

Running off the road at Carol's surprises had become a normal event. "Still want me to go with you?" she asked.

Even Little Mutt raised her head from my lap and looked over at Carol. "What will your 'heathen' girlfriends say?"

"Oh , they think it's a marvelous idea."

"And your mother?"

"Her, too." Carol reached over and touched my shoulder. "Before you ask, Sam's onboard as well."

Wow! I thought. My mind raced. Three whole days in California with Carol, a place neither of us had ever been; another first in the chapter that we were beginning to write. "I'll make the plane reservations in the morning."

"There's only one thing," she added.

"Anything's fine with me," I said, my smile turning into a wide grin.

"We'll have to have separate rooms."

"No problem."

Chapter
66

CAROL AND I had finally set the day of February 26, a Sunday, for our wedding. But on the flight out, we'd considered doing it while we were in Napa. Logistics, and the fact that her mother had told her that she would kill Carol if she did not finally have the chance to witness her daughter getting married, heavily influenced our decision to wait.

It seemed from the time of our first non-date, Carol and I were being constantly sprinkled by Tinker Bell and her magic dust. San Francisco and Napa would be no exception. The next morning, after a ride on a world-famous San Francisco Cable Car, Carol and I met Fred and Bea and headed for Napa.

Fred and Bea do nothing short of first class, and our trip to Napa would be more of the same. Immediately, they hit it off with Carol, and the fun began. The drive up the California Coast into the Napa valley was spectacular. World-class vineyards abound like hog farms in the South. It appears that everyone is in on the act, including movie moguls and actors.

Wine may be the big star in Napa, but its little cousin is mustard with a festival honoring it every year. And, of course, there's food. If there is one place that Food TV could camp forever and still keep an active audience, it would be Napa. From roadside to opulent, this place was a "Foodie's" paradise.

To really enjoy wine, food is a must, and restaurants abound. The first night, we ate at a festive place full of noise and conversation. It was a fun place and the food was wonderful and plentiful.

The second night was totally different. Before we'd even made reservations for a hotel back in November, Bea had tried to get us into a place called *The French Laundry*. It appears that this place is *the* restaurant in all of Northern California. Bea had told me that in order to get a reservation, one had to call exactly ninety days prior to the planned date, and the window of opportunity usually did not stay open for more than fifteen minutes. By the time Bea had gotten through at 8:12 a.m., Pacific Time, the restaurant was full.

The day we'd arrived in San Francisco, while Carol and I waited for our luggage, I'd received a call from Bea that someone had canceled for the night she'd been waitlisted, and that we had ten minutes to accept the reservation with a credit card.

"Why not," I said.

So here we were at this famous place that it seems everybody was dying to get into.

"This place is so quiet it reminds me of a library," I said as we walked into the foyer that doubled as a lobby at the converted two-story house.

"Smells expensive," Fred said, making a dollar sign in the air.

"It's not too late to turn back," I said.

"Not when they've got my credit card number," Bea warned as she followed Fred through the door.

While all the other places in Napa were festive and fun, this place was formal and snobbish. It was so formal that all the waiters wore three-piece Armani suits. Fred is a member of *The Congressional Country Club* and I can assure you that the main dining room there is formal, but it is like eating at the "Tasty Diner" compared to *The French Laundry*.

We had seven or eight courses so small that what the four of us ate that night would have barely filled a normal-sized dinner plate, laid side-to-side. I'll bet that all-total each person got less than six ounces. Was it good? I can't honestly say. I never tasted enough to really tell. One bite just isn't enough to kick-start my taste buds.

Finally, after a couple of hours, the ordeal ended and Mr. Armani presented Fred with the bill.

"What's the verdict?" I asked.

Fred gulped and shook his head.

"That bad?" I asked.

Fred cleared his throat. "If we'd each had more than one glass of wine, we'd have had to take out a mortgage, but what we have here would make a nice monthly payment."

Again I looked at Fred, my eyes asked the question, "How much?"

Rather than answering me, he pushed the leather-bound folder over to me. As I opened it up, my glance took me to the bottom of the page. "I hope this includes the tip."

Fred nodded. "It does."

Keep in mind that I love good food. I love fine dining. But I also love to eat. I hate to leave a place not really knowing what I'd had or not enjoying what I'd had. Couple all that with leaving hungry and the feeling of being ripped off. Talk about the "Emperor's New Clothes." We could have all eaten three meals a day at a *Cracker Barrel* for a month for less money, and at least would have left each time feeling full.

Other than that one night, Napa was a blast. The days were full of wine and fun. The four of us bonded, and I could tell that Fred and Bea really took to Carol. I knew that they would. These two people are almost as close to me as Jimmy and Patti, and although they did not have a vote either, their approval was special.

Finally, it was time to take Carol to the airport. As I faced her departure, emotion drained from me like helium from a balloon. My heart, just hours before so full of excitement and joy that any moment might explode, began to sag and droop. I knew I was going to miss her—terribly.

Since New Year's Eve, we'd seen one another every single day. Now, for the first time since we'd begun our magical flight together, we'd be apart for five whole days. The airport, bustling with people hugging and saying goodbye, reminded me of a train station in some old World War II movie. And just like the main characters from that old black and white movie, we wrapped our arms around each other and kissed goodbye. Slowly, she pulled away from me and at last her finger tips left mine as she drifted away from me and passed through security. Not once did I take my tear-filled eyes off of her. Finally, as she reached the far side of the airport lobby, she turned, blew me a kiss and mouthed, "I love you." But there was something in her eyes that scared me to death. My little voice shook me and warned me that she might not be there when I returned home.

Chapter
67

AROL HAD NEVER BEEN MARRIED. She'd come close a couple of times, but it never happened. Weddings made her so uncomfortable that she rarely attended, even a ceremony for family and close friends. Now, the comment her brother had made when I first met his family began to haunt me. I realized that she'd approached that crossroads again, and although I knew that Carol loved me, I had to make sure that her old demons never had a chance to breathe, let alone surface.

During the five days we were apart, I found time to think and to pray. I knew she loved me. I knew she wanted to marry me. And I knew beyond a shadow of a doubt that I loved her. Over and over in my mind I re-played the scene at the airport. I realized that the look in her eyes had not scared me as much as it had haunted me. I finally came to the conclusion that it was her fear, not mine, and that with God's help I had to make that fear go away.

For most of my life, I'd been a fix-it guy. God knows how many times I wanted to fix Jane's illness and make it go away. I'd found it difficult to place my fears and concerns into God's hands and wait to find out what He wanted for me. Time and time again, when I'd discovered the strength to just let go, He had always shown me the way. But, like many of us, I'd always found that doing that one thing He really wants me to do was as difficult as changing the color of my eyes.

Carol and I talked several times a day during those five days. Not once did her "look" find its way into her voice, yet the haunting continued. We moved on with our plans. She talked about the work being done at the house, the new bedroom furniture she'd bought, and the wedding. Not once had I mentioned how I felt. I kept trying to place it all in God's hands.

"Ah-ha" moments for me have been few and far between. I think it's because I don't listen enough. I now know that Angels speak to us all the time— messages from God delivered in so many ways and forms. My problem has been that to hear them, I had to pay attention, to listen. Instead of listening, I'd always been too busy trying to figure out the problem. On the way home, I stopped in Dallas to change planes. When I arrived, I called to tell Carol that it was snowing in Dallas and that I might be delayed. Her voice and demeanor showed no sign of misgiving, yet that little voice of mine kept nagging away at me.

Before we hung up, she said, "Be careful and come home to me. I love you."

I've been a pilot for many years, and I've probably flown many thousands of miles on commercials airlines. During all that time in and around airports, I've never had the experience of being de-iced. Every time I'd thought of a plane being de-iced, the images brought to life by CNN of the Air Florida crash into the Potomac flashed through my mind. But that day, as I sat buckled up in my seat watching the orange de-icer spray across the fuselage and wings like a high-speed power washer, it came to me.

"Is God in this thing?" I asked myself. "Of course He is," I quickly answered. "He is the one that brought us together and if He is in this, He will make it happen."

I turned away from the window, closed my eyes and sat back. I had my answer and with that answer, a peace washed over me like the warm surf from that stretch of sand where I first kissed Carol.

Six hours later, my friend Martha dropped me off at Carol's house. As I walked up her driveway, I saw the yellow light beaming through the glass on her side door. The light felt warm and inviting. The headlights on Martha's car swept across Carol's house like the life-saving beacon from a lighthouse. Melded together, the two lights formed into a single beam of light, drawing me to her.

Suddenly, she appeared at the door. Bolting up the driveway, I dashed toward her widening smile. As I wrapped her into my arms, I breathed a wave of relief. I was home and Carol was there, just like God had promised.

Chapter
68

HE WEEK BEFORE THE WEDDING flashed by faster than a week at the beach. While in San Francisco, I picked up a couple of Brooks Brothers bow ties for Sam and me to wear, but we still had to pick out matching suits. The painters had finally finished at the house, but furniture had to be re-arranged and there was still one more hurdle that had to be faced. Little Mutt had to meet her new companion.

I've often wondered what went on in their collective minds when we finally put the two dogs together. I think it might have gone something like this.

"Okay, Socker, hop in the car," Carol said as she tugged on his leash. "We're going to check out our new home."

"New home?" Socker cocked his head to one side. "What's wrong with the one we have now?"

On the drive into town, Socker stood perched on the console looking out the windshield. "New house?" he thought. "I'm confused. I know we're getting married, but no one ever said anything about moving. Where in the world is she taking me?"

As Carol pulled into the driveway, she looked over at Socker. "Here we are."

"Where are we?" Socker asked himself as he jumped from the car and ran to the nearest bush to raise his leg and do his business.

"Come on, let me show you the house," Carol said.

Once inside the fence, Socker sniffed out each plant, bush and tree. He checked out the chairs, the charcoal grill and even the chimenea. As he moved around the yard, he said, "Hey, this isn't so shabby. Nice big house right on the golf course. Man, I can even see the river from here. I might really like this place."

"Come on boy, let's go inside," Carol coaxed.

"You ain't got to call me twice," Socker said as he bolted for the back door. "I need to check this place out."

Once inside, Socker moved about the downstairs, taking in his new digs. "Not bad. Formal dining room, and look at that kitchen. Oh boy, a fireplace, I can just see myself curled up in front of that thing on a cold winter night. And look at that sun porch. The windows go almost all the way to the floor. I can see out and bark at anyone who passes by. Man, I'm really going to like living here. Best of all, it's all mine. Oh well. Mine with Carol and Sam, And, oh yeah, that new guy Skip." Socker's little button of a tail wagged so fast it blurred. "I think this is going to be okay."

"And who, pray tell, are you?" Little Mutt said as she pranced around the corner.

"Huh?" Socker's tail jolted to a stop in mid-wag.

"Huh?" Little Mutt said as she slowly examined her visitor. "Huh? Is all you have to say? What are you doing in my house?"

"It's my house." Socker stood his ground. "Carol just brought me over to show it to me. We're marrying Skip, you know."

"Carol never told me about you moving in." Little Mutt darted her eyes over at Carol who sat on the couch flipping through a magazine. "I had to get used to

Thumper leaving, then Jane leaving, and finally I get Skip all to myself. Of course, Carol and Sam are pretty cool and I really like them, but nobody told me I'd have to share with someone like you."

"If I can't live here, what am I going to do? It looks like there's plenty of room for us all." Socker's eyes drooped. He lowered his head, turned and lumbered for the door.

"Wait, wait, wait!" Little Mutt said. "Okay, I'm really not that bitchy. I'm sure that in time you'll find that I'm pretty nurturing. I eat on this side of the kitchen, you'll have to get used to the other side."

"You mean, you mean," Socker stuttered as his button tail started to blur again. "You mean I can stay?"

"If Carol, Skip, and Sam like you. I'm sure I will, too. Welcome to your new home. Oh yeah, by the way, I've never seen a dog like you before. What are you?"

Socker's ears perked up. "I'm a Rat Terrier. And you? I've never seen a dog like you, either. Heck, you kind of look like a cat."

"Don't push your luck, buster. I'm a Pekingese. Oh yes, and I am AKC registered," Little Mutt said as she turned and sashayed from the room.

Chapter
69

*O*N SUNDAY MORNING, February 26, 2006, I awoke just as the sun broke through my bedroom window. Suddenly, I felt Little Mutt stretch and leave her spot at the end of the bed. As I rolled back the covers, my precious little dog curled up next to me, snuggling against my arm, a routine we'd continued ever since the day I'd returned from Chapel Hill. As we cuddled together, my mind drifted back to that morning almost four years before when I'd awakened on the couch and felt the warmth of her against me.

But this day was different. Instead of being awakened by what I thought might have been an angel, this morning, I was sure that there were angels all around us. Instead of facing a journey that would take me on a roller coaster ride into the darkest days of my life, this morning would lead to that new chapter Carol and I had started on New Year's Eve.

"Little Mutt," I said as I stroked her head, "we're getting married today." Little Mutt rolled her bright brown eyes up at me as if she'd understood everything I'd said.

Before we left for our morning walk, I checked my email and found a note from Carol. Quickly, I shot her back a reply and took Little Mutt outside. The crisp morning felt good. Overhead, the sunlight reflected off the passenger jets like fireflies on a spring afternoon as they winged their way south. As we walked along the golf course, the frost from the night before reflecting in the morning light made the grass look like a sea of diamonds. I felt at one with the world. It was like a spell had been cast over me, one that I never wanted broken.

By the time I got to Temple Baptist Church for the second service, I found Carol waiting for me in the narthex. "How're you feeling?" I asked.

"Like there's a team of acrobats doing somersaults in my stomach," she replied.

"I'd be lying if I said you don't look nervous." I grabbed her hand and led Carol into the sanctuary. "How'd you sleep?"

"Okay," she stuttered as she found a place for us to sit.

Again, my little voice started to whisper in my ear. I brushed it off. *Get out of here,* I thought.

Shortly, Sam and Jane joined us in the pew and we slid over. Within seconds, the other side filled in leaving Carol wedged in the middle. Carol got quiet and fidgety. Finally, she looked at me. "I've got to get out of here."

I stood up and followed her to the aisle. "You leaving?" I asked. Before she could answer, I took Carol aside. "Go if you have to. But if you don't show up here at two o'clock this afternoon, I'm going to join Temple Baptist Church and sit right behind you every Sunday for the rest of your life."

Carol's eyes lit up and she began to smile. Her smile quickly turned to laughter. "I'm not going anywhere. I just need to have an aisle seat. My claustrophobia is kicking my butt sitting there in the middle."

Halfway through the service, Carol pulled me close and whispered in my ear, "You really meant what you said about sitting behind me in church for the rest of my life, didn't you?"

"You damn right," I answered.

263

"Not in church," she said, referring to my expletive. Our smiles turned into laughter.

After church at Temple Baptist, Carol elected not to go to my church, Garber United Methodist, suggesting that she needed some time to get ready. For me, the rest of my morning was fuzzy at best. I do remember sitting with Jimmy and Patti at church and the ovation I got from the congregation when I announced during prayer and celebration that Carol and I were getting married that afternoon. I also remember that I ate lunch at the club, shoveling the meal down so fast that moments later, I didn't remember what I'd eaten.

Good friends are those we can rely on in our time of need, and for the past several years, I'd relied heavily on my friends. That day, as I got dressed in my wedding suit, I realized this day would be no different.

"Hello," Jimmy said as he picked up the phone.

"Jimmy, I'm in trouble," I said, my voice changing octaves as I spoke. "That little thing, you know the one that's supposed to keep people from stealing stuff from a store, you know that plastic thing. It's still on my suit jacket. They didn't take it off, and if I try, it will explode, or something. Man, I'm in real trouble. I don't know what to do. I'm supposed to be at the church in fifteen minutes, but I've got to get this thing off."

"Slow down," Jimmy ordered. "What are you talking about?"

"You know, that plastic thing that they put on coats and jackets."

"Oh yeah, what about it?" Jimmy asked.

"At the store, somehow they didn't take it off, and I don't have time to take it back. Oh my God they might not be open on Sunday. What am I going to do?"

"Calm down. We're on our way over," he said followed by a click on the other end.

WITH PATTI AND JIMMY on their way to the department store to rescue my suit jacket, I pulled up in front of the church. For a moment, the thought of someone trashing my car crossed my mind, but Carol and I were not twenty-two and hopefully our friends had set aside those sophomoric gestures we'd loved to participate in many years before.

Inside, Carol's brother Merril and his wife Bridgett had already found a spot up front. My nephew, Walt, and Carol's nephew, Bobby—our ushers—showed up and started to seat the early arrivals. Shortly, others trickled in, and I found my way to pastor Steve Cobb's office.

Steve Cobb is the best "pulpit" preacher I have ever heard. A man in his late forties, with an Ashville, North Carolina, accent, this six-foot-two marathon runner has a dominating presence in front of an audience that overshadows his natural shyness. On most Sunday mornings, he will be found dressed for church in a knit shirt and sport coat. Finding him in a double breasted suit and tie, a page out of GQ Magazine, surprised me. As we stood outside of his office, I noticed Pastor Powell making his way through the church. "I thought you said this was going to be a small wedding," he jested. "I almost couldn't find a place to park."

"Just family and friends." I reached out and shook his hand. "But, you know, Carol's related to almost everyone in western Craven County."

When the time came, Steve led us to an anteroom just off the sanctuary. I peeped through the door and Powell was right. This wasn't a small crowd. But the people who counted were there. Our friends and family had come in force to support our union, but seeing Debbie and Glenn and their families was the icing on the cake.

Finally, after listening through the door to Carol's niece Tammy singing one of my favorite hymns, "Surely

The Spirit of The Lord is in This Place," a lifetime of waiting came to an end as the organist struck the first cords of *Cannon D.* The two ministers and I walked into the sanctuary and took our place at the chancel. All eyes were on Carol as she and Sam slowly made their way down the aisle. She looked scared to death. Her eyes had that "deer in the headlights" look, and the two red roses she held in her hands trembled.

When Steve Cobb asked, "Who gives this woman to this man?"

Sam answered, "I do." After placing Carol's hand in mine, Sam stepped over beside me and took his place as my best man.

A few promises later, Steve introduced us as husband and wife. As we left the altar, Carol and I each gave one of the roses she'd carried to our mothers before we made our way to the narthex. For Carol, the trembling had stopped, the fear was over. Our life together had begun.

Life After Death

PART FIVE

*"Anyone can become a father,
but not everyone can be a dad."*

Chapter
70

*F*OR CAROL AND ME, the first year flew by almost as fast as our courtship. Part of our daily routine was a brisk morning walk. Walks on the golf course in the spring can be nothing short of spectacular; budding dogwoods and azaleas share the stage with wisteria and periwinkle. Purples and yellows and whites and reds compete with greens and blues. Things were coming alive one April morning when we finished our walk.

"Skip, I've been thinking about something." Carol stopped, turned and looked me in the eyes. "You and Sam have bonded beyond my wildest dream. Have you ever thought about adopting him?"

My throat suddenly dried up and my eyes swelled. Sam had been one of the reasons that we'd decided to get married when we did. I remember telling Carol when we were dating that when she took Sam off to college that I wanted to be with her so that she would have someone to drive her back home. I knew how much she would miss him. I never thought that she'd be the one driving me back home from Campbell University that August Saturday—my tears flowing the whole way back.

Sam had become the son I'd always wanted. Our bond had developed into something huge. From the beginning, I'd always introduced him as my son, never my stepson. I always wanted him to be a part of what Carol and I shared, and as we spent more and more time together, little things like him referring to us as his "parents" became so special to me. We shared so much and had even more in common. We both loved boating, and fishing, sports—especially football—food, travel, politics and on and on. I can't remember anything that one of us had an interest in that the other didn't have as well. And now, for Carol to suggest that I might want to adopt Sam...for me that was a given.

"Carol, you won't believe what I'm getting ready to tell you," I said. "I've been wondering for about a month how you might feel about making Sam 'our' son. I've even talked with some folks at the County Clerk's office, and since Sam's birthfather is deceased, all it will take is a copy of the death certificate and your consent—and, of course, Sam's."

"That seems pretty simple," Carol said, grabbing my hand as we continued our walk.

"Since Sam is over eighteen, it could be done in four days or less. Have you talked with him about it?"

"No, I haven't. But I know how much he loves and respects you. I'm sure he'd be tickled."

I stopped again and this time I looked into Carol's eyes. "What if he doesn't want to? That would put a ton of pressure on him."

"Let me talk with him," Carol said. "I'll kinda feel him out before you say anything."

"It needs to come from me. Sam needs to know it's my idea." I scratched my chin and pursed my lips. "Then when he's ready, he'll see how you feel."

"Makes sense to me," Carol said. "When do you think you'll ask him?"

"I'm going to do some praying and thinking. He comes home this weekend and maybe that's when I'll ask him. But the moment has to be the right one."

Within a few days, I'd made up my mind that I'd ask Sam that weekend, probably on Sunday. I wanted to ask him just before he left for school, when he'd have a couple of hours to just think about it during the drive back.

As Sam prepared to go back to school, I followed him to his car and broke the question. "Sam," I stammered. "I was thinking how great it has been for us this past year and I am wondering if you'd let me adopt you. Before you answer, let me say that I've talked with Carol and she's all for it. You won't have to change your name, you'll always be Sam Dail, but you'll be my son forever. That means, that you will be heir to whatever I've set aside, you'll be listed in all the Crayton and Dalrymple genealogy as my son, not my stepson, or my adopted son, but the son of Paul Washington Crayton, Jr. and Carol Dail Crayton. Walt, Anna, and Jenna will be your first cousins, and Grandma Flossie will be your real grandmother."

Sam smiled and nodded as I continued.

"Sam, you don't have to answer me today. Take all the time you need. If this is something that you feel uncomfortable with or don't want to do, you don't have to tell me no. Just don't bring it up. I can assure you that I love you and that adopting you will never make me love you more. Whatever happens, that love I have for you will never change, no matter what you decide."

Sam reached out and shook my hand. Nodding he said, "Thanks, I'll think about it."

Two weeks passed and I asked Carol if she'd heard from Sam. She told me that he'd talked with her, but she didn't have a clue about his decision. Three weeks passed and still nothing. I figured that he might have decided to leave things as they were so I placed it in God's hands.

On Father's Day, Carol, Sam and Jane, along with my mother and Carol's mom, took me to the country club for lunch after church. At the end of the meal, Carol presented me with several cards, and, as always, I opened cards from all our dogs and cats. When I'd finished, Sam looked over at me and said, "There's one more."

271

I slowly opened the card from Sam. I never got to the verse. All I saw was: *The answer is yes. I love you...Sam.* I lost it in the main dining room of the New Bern Golf and Country Club.

Four days later, as I drove toward the County Clerk's Office, I turned on my radio. *Color Him Father* by the Winstons was playing, a gift from God. That afternoon, I became Sam's dad.

Epilogue

*I*T'S BEEN FOUR YEARS since I met Sam and Carol at the clerk of the court's office, and Carol and I just celebrated our fifth anniversary. To say that our lives have changed would be like saying that from time-to-time, it gets hot in August—a huge understatement. In fact, one of Carol's favorite sayings is, "Girl, you are not in Kansas anymore," referring to all the changes that came her way when she hooked up with me.

We are a family in every sense of the word, and I wouldn't have it any other way. Sam and I have bonded far beyond anything I could have dreamed. I know he loves me and that he respects me. He shows how he feels in so many small ways. It has been said that imitation is the greatest form of flattery and Sam flatters me all the time, from having to have an old StarTech cell phone like mine to posing for a picture in Jamaica dressed like me in the same spot. I pray every day that I will never let him down and that I can set an example that he will want to follow.

Our life is not exciting to anyone but us, however the pure excitement of being a family makes our life together so special. Now, when the Dail family—we had thirty-four over for Thanksgiving this year—or the Crayton crowd gets together, we are our own family unit. We have all been accepted into each of those families. It has become second nature for Walt, Anna, and Jenna to introduce Sam as their first cousin and for all the nephews and nieces on Carol's side to call me

Uncle Skip. It is as if we've all been together for a lifetime.

Sam graduated from Campbell in May of 2010 with honors. He applied for medical school at UNC, ECU and Marshall. All told him to try again in a year. At ECU, they sat down with Sam and told him what he needed to do to get in. Part of that was to enroll in the public health master's program at East Carolina along with a suggested list of volunteering opportunities that would help his cause.

So that's what he did. For a year, he followed the advice of those doctors at the ECU med school and reapplied to the one school he wanted to attend. On our anniversary this year, Sam got the letter we'd all been praying for. He starts in August as a first-year medical student at the Brody School of Medicine at ECU.

Little Mutt and Socker are still with us, albeit both are a little slower these days. But the bond they formed that first day they met has grown into a vast friendship. And now they have a new addition to break in. Last year, Sam's graduation present was a white standard Poodle named Bodie. (I call her miss Wide Open.) Little Mutt and Socker have had their paws full.

And now Carol and I are getting a daughter. Exactly one week after his acceptance into medical school, Sam got down on one knee and asked his Jane to marry him. On her hand he placed a ring. The center stone on Jane Moon's engagement ring is the same diamond that my father and I picked out for the ring that I gave to Jane Crayton in August of 1967, a ring she wore for more than thirty-eight years.

Our love for one another is steadfast and strong. In five years, Carol and I have not had one cross word between us. As close to perfect as things have been for us, just like with everyone, life still throws curve balls at us from time to time. God did not promise us that life would be a bed of roses, and it is how we deal with those rough times that really matters; we either run away, try to fix things ourselves, or we give them to God.

Jesus said in John 16:33 *"I have told you these things, so that in me you may have peace. In this world you will have trouble. But take heart! I have overcome the world."* (NIV) And in Proverbs 3:5-6 The Bible states *5 Trust in the LORD with all your heart and lean not on your own understanding; 6 in all your ways submit to Him, and He will direct your paths.* (NIV)

It was never my plan for this book to be "preachy," but hopefully to be inspirational. I had not planned to quote scripture, but the quote from Proverbs reared up and slapped me across the face. I was taken away by it during a sermon and it gnawed at me for days. I eventually mentioned to Carol that I thought that I might use that one quote as I felt it echoed the message that I was trying to tell.

Just before Carol retires, she reads the Bible. Lately, she's been reading Jane's study Bible. One night as I was in my office pondering the use of scripture, she asked me to come into our bedroom. As I walked into the room, Carol said, "There's something you need to see." She handed me Jane's Bible, turned to Proverbs 3. My heart flew to my throat as I looked at the page. On the page only two verses had been highlighted—both jumped out at me like a bright yellow neon sign. Jane had highlighted verses 5 and 6. I felt that I had been sent a message from Heaven—angels speaking to me again.

We still go to two churches on Sunday; Temple Baptist at nine o'clock and Garber Methodist at eleven o'clock. That schedule doesn't allow for a Sunday school class, but hey, we've got the best teacher anyone could want in Steve Cobb.

So each morning as I walk out the door so that Little Mutt and Socker can take me for our walk, I first thank

God for the wonderful day He's provided. As I say my prayers, I ask Him to show me how I can better serve Him that day, and I pray that whatever happens to me that day that I can truly turn it all over to Him. It is a lesson I work on every day of my life. Maybe that's a part of why He picked me up and carried me into the light and gave me "Life after Death."

Some Final Thoughts

*S*O, WHY DID I WRITE THIS STORY? My story? Why was I *driven* to write it? Was it to feed my ego? Was it to make me feel good? Was it for a pat on the back for finding triumph over tragedy? Was it another try for a best seller? I hope not.

I never wanted this story to be sappy or self-indulgent. And whether it sells one copy or five million has nothing to do with my reason for writing it. My hope was to write something that would touch those in similar depths of despair to know that there is hope, that there is light, and that that light comes from God.

Just like with most couples, Jane and I had a far-from-perfect marriage. In fact, we almost separated after twenty years together, but thanks to a wonderful counselor, who showed us how to love that hurt child that lives within us all, we overcame our differences. By saving ourselves, we saved our marriage as well. Those remaining years were some of the best years we spent together, but as strange as it may seem, they were not the very best.

Those years came during Jane's illness, after the vision she had when she was in the coma—the vision that brought us both back to God. I truly believe He showed us the way back for a purpose. I believe that Jane's mission was to testify for God and show how He changes lives.

Life is much different for Carol and me. She and Jane are as different as sea and sky. For much of her life, Jane could have been characterized as "high maintenance," while Carol is fiercely independent, something that really attracted me to her. Unlike what we used to call the three-minute rule where if I was idle for three minutes, Jane would find something for me to do, Carol gives me vast freedom. She lets me be who I am, yet trusts me to a fault. Her love is like the open door on a bird cage. I have the freedom to go as far as I want, but because of that love I never drift far from the nest.

There is one theme that I've tried to permeate throughout this story and that is the one of God's determination. Some say that God moves in mysterious ways, and for most of us, that is an easy explanation. But I think that there is more. I believe that God works in *determined* ways. It is His determination that all His children find their way to Him. There is nothing random about God or His will. I don't think for one minute that Carol, Sam, and I are together by chance. There is no mystery as to why we are together. All we have to do is pay attention and listen.

That Jane, and Sam's birthfather, Billy, have gone to be with God, is far from a mystery. It is all part of God's plan for us; His determination, for reasons only He knows, that the three of us are together at this time. Did God take Jane and Billy in order for us to be together? No. But there is one thing I know for sure: they are in a much better place. God was ready for them to be with Him.

And there's one more thing that I'm certain of, as Carol reminded me on that wonderful New Year's Eve: God does not make mistakes. We are all where we are because it is part of His plan and His determined will to bring us all to Him.

Most of my life and even today with all I've been through and have observed, I still have difficulty trusting in God. I'm always trying to fix things.

However, now I try to place more attention and emphasis on leaving it all in God's hands. That may be the most difficult process we all need to learn. Carol reminds me daily to give it all to God and that He will show us the way. And what was it that Jane said in her testimony? "God, I lay it all at your feet."

As I look back at my journey out of the darkness, I experienced most of the symptoms of personal tragedy: despair, fear, and loneliness. Yet, the one symptom that never took hold of me was anger, and especially anger at God. I knew that for me to get through the pain and suffering, I would not be able to make it without Him. There were times He sent my friends to help me, times He walked beside me, and times He carried me, but He was always there.

Maybe if there is one theme I want to convey, it is this: Trust in God and He will provide. You might not like the direction He is taking you, but when it is all said and done, you will be exactly where He wants you to be.

Will there be times of trouble ahead for all of us? There is no question that there will be. God never promised us total peace and happiness here on earth. That is to come at a later time. Jane, Billy, and all those we've loved who've passed on before us are already experiencing it. But God has promised us one thing: He will be with us...even to the end of the earth.

ONE FINAL THOUGHT: and what about the angels?

Throughout this story, I mention angels. For most of my life I've never understood angels. The Bible has very little to say about them, yet every theologian that reviewed my story told me that they are very real, indeed. As much as I've written about angels, it has been only recently that I understood who or what they are and how they function in our lives. Understanding angels and their presence in our lives came to me like a major "ah-ha" moment.

The way I see it, angels are messengers from God. They are all around us all the time. They speak to us all the time, constantly trying to get our attention. Their messages can be as subtle as a flashing thought or as startling as the "sound" that woke me that Sunday morning in June.

They may speak to us through a song or paint us a brilliant sunset. We may feel their breath on our cheeks like a wisp of wind on a summer day or a sudden feeling of warmth on a January morning. They may speak to us through two co-workers talking in a copy room about a Christmas Ball. Or, in what I believe was the case with the family in the emergency room and the couple on Sam's birthday, if they choose; they may actually appear before us.

But for us to hear what angels are saying, we have to pay attention. I think the reason that I'd spent most of my life wondering if angels existed, is due to the fact that I just didn't listen. But during the journey out of the darkest time of my life, I heard them loud and clear. I know that angels were around me, and along with God and my friends, there to help carry me into the light, to help show me the way. And I pray every day that I'll keep paying attention to the angels, listening for those messages from God.